To my Granddaughter ♡
& love from one
non-girlie-girlr to another.
Grandma Hgel

A GIFT FOR

FROM

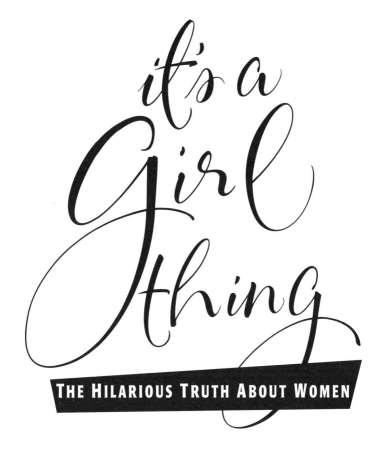

it's a Girl thing

THE HILARIOUS TRUTH ABOUT WOMEN

JAN KING

Andrews McMeel
Publishing

BOK4072

It's a Girl Thing

This edition published in 2002 by Andrews McMeel Publishing
exclusively for Hallmark Cards, Inc.

www.hallmark.com

Book design by Holly Camerlinck

This book is dedicated to all the "girls" in my family who enrich my life every single day with their unconditional love and support.

My Mom
Betty Prahovic

My Sister
Karen Arledge

My Sister-in-Law
Ginny Lasko

My Niece
Jennifer Lasko-Allen

My Great-niece
Genevieve Allen

My Daughter-in-Law
Whitney King

My Stepdaughters
Jennifer Schwarz
Julie Chutick
Jillian Chutick

And My Precious Baby Granddaughter
Sarah Catherine King

CONTENTS

Contents

Contents

ACKNOWLEDGMENTS

There is no doubt that I have THE BEST girlfriends in the world. They constantly make me laugh and generously share their girl stories, which eventually end up in my books. Naturally, I change the names to protect the guilty. So here's to my gal-pals.

East Coast Girlfriends	West Coast Girlfriends
Karyn Byrne	Glo Heller
Jan Rainbolt	Nancy Johnson
Catherine Mann-Grandy	Wendy Greene
Margaret Herrmann	Elizabeth Jackson
Rudi Stryker	Karen Rosales
Lyne Weiss	Caroline Sweet
Hannah Piteo	Meredith Schirmer
Carlynn Donosky	Julie Hayworth
Carole Blum	Becky Borg
Marilyn Taylor	Cyndy Purcell
Yasmin Choudhry	Roberta Isgreen
Shahrzad Miller	Sandy Richter
Rita Martin	Nurit Lovi

And the Guys

To my husband, Mark Chutick, who has always been my number one supporter and has been responsible for making all of my dreams come true, I love you. Thank you for your unwavering belief in my talent and your encouragement over the years. I couldn't do any of it without you.

To my friend Jon Anderson, there's no way I can thank you enough for the assistance and advice you've so generously given to help further my career as a writer throughout the years. I am fortunate to know a person of such integrity and honesty, and I treasure our friendship.

To my editor, Allan Stark, thank you for all your wisdom and encouragement and for providing the vehicle for me to reach countless women out there to give them a few well-deserved chuckles.

To my sons, Michael and Philip, you both are, beyond a doubt, the best creations I ever produced. I love you very much and am so proud of the fine young men you have both become.

INTRODUCTION

I t's a *Girl Thing* takes on the Herculean task of explaining the many mind-boggling idiosyncrasies of female behavior. It's a well-known fact that these loopy behaviors are what separate the girls from the boys. Therefore, it would be completely redundant to add that this is a humor book. But I'll say it anyway, just for that one person in the universe who has spent his entire life in his freezer.

Because there are so many "girl things" that ultimately define women's behavior, I have meticulously chronicled them so they may be researched by great minds who specialize in studying the female species, like David Hasselhoff. This is the kind of book that women will read and laughingly say, "Omigod—that's me!!!" Men would be smart if they read it, too. It could help explain mysteries that are even more arcane than the whereabouts of Jimmy Hoffa's body.

The truth is that women have no real control over their compulsive tendencies because they are predetermined by our "girl genes." These genes are responsible for all the inherent peculiarities of our species, like nail-polish fetishes, pumping collagen into every depression on our bodies, overpacking for trips, changing our hair color weekly, spending a year's salary on Tupperware products, and serving soybeans as an entrée.

Since the dawn of existence, men have never understood why women do the things we do. This is because males don't have the same complex DNA as women. They only have two genes on their chromosomes determining their basic requirements for survival: sex and barbecue sauce.

ONE

Chick-flicks:

Ten-Hanky Movies

WHAT WOMAN HASN'T SAID TO HER FAMILY, in a voice choked with emotion, at least four gazillion times during her lifetime, "All I want is to be happy."

And the family members, nodding sympathetically as if understanding her pain, are all thinking, "What the hell is she talking about?" This is exactly why we women feel our husbands and kids are part of that "extreme right-wing conspiracy"[1] that continually puts up roadblocks on our way to Sunnybrook Farm. So why is it that for amusement we choose to attend movies that are so depressing and gut wrenching, we sob our hearts out for two hours and dwell in abject misery for weeks afterward? Is this what we want to do to make ourselves "happy"? If so, do we enjoy menstrual cramps as well?

We are all familiar with the genre known as "women's movies," or "chick-flicks." We have flocked in record numbers to such classics as *Terms of Endearment, The English Patient, Beaches, Love Story,* and *Stepmom.* And we have cried so hard that we left the theater with more mascara running down our cheeks than Tammy Faye Bakker at a revival meeting. These movies go way beyond your ordinary "tear jerkers." They are the sort of movies that elicit aerobic-level sobs and leave you prostrate spanning six seats.

Why do we subject ourselves to the kinds of movies that men instinctively run from at warp speed? If you even mention a movie like *Beaches* to a guy, he will beg off with every excuse in the book, from enlisting in the Israeli army to being scheduled for prostate surgery. You might think that guys are much smarter

---

1. The same group that slipped the Havana cigars into Clinton's humidor.

than women for not subjecting themselves to such depressing cinematic sagas. However, after turning down *Beaches,* men will rush out to see a picture like *Extreme Ninjas,* where they thrive on such bloody spectacles as guys getting knifed through the heart, getting shot through the brains, or having their eyeballs pop out of their sockets from strangulation. Go figure.

But returning to our original question: Why do women crave movies that make them so sad? What makes us so fascinated by everybody else's death? Why are we irresistibly drawn to such stories like Buttafuoco to jailbait? I'll be damned if I know. But one thing I do know is that all these sob movies have predictable "cookbook deaths" that all follow one of a small number of basic story lines:

1. The "You can see it coming" death: The heroine is always diagnosed with some rare terminal illness during the first half hour of the movie, after which it takes her approximately 7.6 boxes of Kleenex to die. And the rarer the illness, the better. If it's a brain tumor, it's never just your ordinary garden-variety type of tumor. It has to be like the one Bette Davis had in *Dark Victory,* in which she had six months of robust health following diagnosis but then went blind, deaf, and incontinent all in the final five minutes of the movie.

2. The "I didn't see it coming" death: This generally takes place when the heroine's entire family is wiped out in the blink of an eye through a freak accident, like being mowed down by a renegade snowmobile on the slopes of a trendy ski resort, such as Gstaad. Or sometimes, the family members meet their untimely demises on separate occasions from a deranged serial killer like Hannibal Lecter, who is posing as the family's trusted attorney. The family is executed, one by one, after inviting him to dinner, where they make the fatal mistake of serving him fava beans and a bottle of *bad* Chianti.

3. The "Watch out for the plot twist" death: This familiar type of plot entails a woman's daughter being run down and killed by a drunk driver. This is a man who doesn't have one single redeeming quality except perhaps his ability to whistle "Strangers in the Night" through his nose. But as he lies dying from injuries sustained in the accident, the mother valiantly and unselfishly decides to donate all of the daughter's organs (including her ovaries) to save the bum's life. Then the perp goes on to repent by praying for ten years in a monastery, wearing nothing but a hairshirt and a pair of Just My Size pantyhose.

When he returns to the outside world, he courts

and marries the woman who donated her daughter's organs to him. Nine months later, after they both become pregnant, they simultaneously deliver twins. Naturally, one is good and the other evil.

FROM YEARS OF EXPERIENCE, I know the signs that mean you'll need to start digging the tissues out of your purse. The first is the mention of a LUMP of any kind. Lumps in the head, the legs, or even in gravy are *always* a bad sign. A small lump that starts out as a harmless ingrown hair will eventually turn into a wildly malignant growth the size of a small weather balloon. Trust me. Didn't Debra Winger start out with a little pimple on her armpit in *Terms*? And look what that turned into.

Pale is another bad omen. And paleness coupled with under-eye circles spells certain death. Remember the pale-skinned, dark-eyed Jennie in *Love Story*? Doomed as doomed can be. The medical treatment she got was bad enough, but the script treatment was even worse. She died tragically, and she wasn't even an HMO patient.

And speaking of long, drawn-out deaths, *The English Patient* is a perfect example. Whenever there is a love triangle with incredibly hot and steamy sex that satisfies the lovers down to their adrenal glands, it's always the female (playing the hypotenuse) who "gets it" in the end. This is the way Hollywood works. The price a woman has to pay for having sex with wild abandon is not just your regular run-of-the-mill death. It has to be really sadistic. This one had Kristin Scott Thomas starving in a remote cave for weeks without so much as a hotplate.

Another storyline that is sure to produce more blubber than Moby Dick is the star-crossed-lover scenario. Hundreds of famous couples throughout history have fallen into this category, but the most memorable are:

Napoleon and Josephine
Romeo and Juliet
Antony and Cleopatra
Cher and Greg Allman

But the most star-crossed pair of them all was Barbra Streisand and Robert Redford in the cinematic sobfest *The Way We Were*. Women are still crying over that heart-wrenching split-up, twenty years after it happened. I think what gets us more than anything else is that we will never understand exactly why their marriage broke up. We are still asking ourselves, "What happened? They were so gorgeous together."

I guess that's a question that will be pondered by Rhodes scholars until the end of time. Maybe it was a cultural thing—the age-old clash of chopped liver versus caviar that was just too wide a gap to bridge. But still, they had everything going for themselves. They loved each other. They were intellectual equals. Their sex was hotter than Jennifer Lopez's Golden Globes gown. He must have been nuts. She was definitely meshugge.

I guess in retrospect, the fault had to lie with the Jewish-Christian thing. The man was just too haymisha for his own good. Maybe he should have gone shopping with her more often. Maybe she should have taken up fly-fishing to please him. Maybe he didn't find kosher food all that geshmakta. Isn't it amazing what havoc one little gefilte fish can wreak in a marriage?

Just recently, Hollywood has put another knife in the heart of every young mother with the movie *Stepmom*. It expertly plays on the worst fear that every mother on earth holds. And it's not just the fact that she might die. We all expect that to happen one day. It's that she might die *and then* be replaced by Julia Roberts. Hollywood can be so cruel.

They could have used Bea Arthur or even Cyndi Lauper in the role of the stepmom. But noooooo. It had to be a woman half our age, with a perfect body, perfect teeth, and hair so thick it doesn't even need volumizer. In my opinion, they knocked off the wrong woman. Julia Roberts should have been the one to bite the dust, not Susan Sarandon. But those young male screenwriters just can't resist killing off a middle-aged woman with crow's feet and cellulite, who's also having a bad hair day. Now, this is something to really cry about.

TWO

Big Girls Do Cry:

Tears on My Pillow

I
T'S NO SECRET that women have the singular ability to cry at the drop of a hat. Our emotions always run right under the surface, bubbling over at the slightest provocation. However, women do this weird thing. When we're caught crying, we always deny it. When questioned, we all recite the same pat answer: "Me—crying? Don't be silly. It's my allergies."

Somebody would make a fortune if they marketed an "I Can't Believe I'm Not Crying" kit, filled with items that make red, swollen eyes look normal or at least camouflage them. Then, after you've finished using the products, you can hyperventilate into the empty bag. A woman could take it to the movies, weddings, or just about anyplace where she's likely to suffer an "allergy attack." The kit would contain:

Cucumber slices
Tea bags
Sunglasses
Visine
Wite-Out

People need to understand that they must never interfere when a woman cries. We need to cry for our emotional well-being. If you interrupt a woman while she is crying, something really terrible will happen. No, she won't shoot herself. It's worse than that. She'll start retaining fluid—gallons of it. Blow up bigger than Pavarotti.

It's a curious thing about women. No matter what emotion they're feeling, they express it by turning on the waterworks. Women don't cry only when we're sad. We cry when we're happy, angry, afraid, or just because we're feeling sorry for ourselves. But we seldom shed tears in response to the actual event. For example, when we are crying at the movies, it's rarely about what's taking place on the screen. Instead, we're crying over "stuff" that has been eating at our insides for the past thirty years. You know just what I'm talking about. "Stuff" like:

When you didn't get asked to the junior prom

Losing at cheerleader tryouts

All the birthdays and anniversaries your husband forgot

Your cat getting run over when you were in the third grade

That undeserved F you got in college physics

There are also specific times when we go through periods of being weepy, like when we're experiencing PMS.[1] This is when anything—and I mean anything—can make you lose it. Husbands have learned from bitter experience to keep a safe distance[2] from their wives when they're suffering with PMS. A husband might make an innocent remark like, "Honey, you have a spot on your blouse." Your response might be to dissolve into a pool of tears—or swallow a bottle of Drano. You never know with this condition.

It's easy for guys. They solve all their hormonal midlife crises by dating younger women and buying

---

1. Thirty days a month.

2. The next state would be their best bet.

Harleys. But women don't go down this highway. We face our midlife problems much more realistically. First we get a facelift, and then we redecorate the entire house. But take it from me, women have a lot to cry about at middle age. Things like:

The cruel lighting in dressing rooms

Being referred to as "Ma'am" instead of "Miss"

Our boobs getting closer to our waists

Having to wear Hush Puppies with our cocktail dresses

Hormonal mustaches

Wait—there's more: the category of nonfilm productions capable of generating more tears than a guest on Jerry Springer who finds out the girl he's married to is actually his brother.[3] These are family productions involving our children, a stage, and anything that might remotely resemble a script. Any mother will attest to the fact that when it comes to watching our kids perform, we dissolve into one slobbering mass of female protoplasm.

I remember the time when my son was cast as one of the "snowflakes" in the second-grade production *The Story of Winter.* When I saw him up there in his sheet cut

---

3. And this is *before* the sex change operation.

out like a snowflake with his darling little blue lips reciting his "Brrrrrrrr" line, I was dead meat. Bawled all over the place. Of course he was only one snowflake in a whole blizzard, so it took me most of the play to locate him. But nonetheless, my pride wasn't dampened a bit—only my hanky.

I would be remiss not to include award ceremonies in this lachrymal cavalcade. And watch out. If you haven't experienced the thrill of watching your child receive an award—be prepared. It requires a Turkish towel. During those moments when your daughter gets her Brownie merit badge or your son is chosen MVP for his T-ball league, trust me—*you will lose it*. They will have to carry you out on a stretcher.

Weddings are also multihanky events. Especially when it's your daughter who is getting married. We moms are left dabbing our eyes for months afterward because we have lost our best gal-pal and our house is emptier than a politician's promises. Your husband cries for months, too—but over the astronomical wedding costs, and the belief that his new son-in-law is a total meat-head.

I also believe that women get overly emotional at weddings because by the time our kids are old enough to get married, we realize that we have reached that age where we will forget how to hook our bras. It's hard to believe that the "little kids" who were pooping their diapers just yesterday are walking down the aisle today. Only now it's the parents who are wearing diapers.

Another trait that separates the girls from the boys is the rules about anger. Guys love to get angry. They thrive on fighting. The nastier the better. But women are totally different. We have a real problem expressing anger because from the time we are little girls we were taught that it's not acceptable to show it. Our society calls men who are angry "charismatic" and "macho." But an angry woman is a bitch.[4] It's that simple. No pop psychology necessary here. Just ask Dr. Laura.

When a woman gets angry, she cries. If an argument reaches the point where a woman would like nothing more than to bust a guy's nose, she busts out crying instead. Here's a typical marital spat, showing how this works in practice:

HUSBAND: (*Furious*) Do you know how much our long-distance bill was last month? It was outrageous.

WIFE: (*Indignant*) I have every right to call my mother. She happens to be sick.

---

4. And that's the flattering term.

HUSBAND: (*Sarcastic*) So write her letters from now on.

WIFE: (*Getting a lump in her throat*) Listen to me, buster, and listen good. If you ever tell me what I can or can't do again I'm going to whaaaaaaaaaaaaaaaa . . .

Can we help it if we start wailing like a baby? Don't forget, we grew up watching Lucy do it to Ricky every week. Besides, crying serves two valuable purposes:

1. It releases tension.
2. It makes men feel guiltier than Hugh Grant.[5]

Crying is also a brilliant tactical strategy to find out things that your significant other would otherwise never tell you. It helps keep men off guard because they never know what's going on inside that head of yours. That's what's known as a home-court advantage. Case in point: Your significant other presents you with a beautiful nightgown for your birthday. You burst into tears of joy.

HE: What's the matter, honey? Don't you like it?

---

5. *After* he got caught.

SHE: Sob, sob—no, that's not it.

HE: It's real silk. I paid $300 for it.

SHE: Sob, sob—no, that's not why I'm crying.

HE: I picked it out for you at Victoria's Secret. My secretary even modeled it for me to help make up my mind.

SHE: She did? Sniffle, sniffle—when?

HE: (*Proudly*) Oh, after I took her out for cocktails last night.

SHE: Whaaaaaaaaaaaaaaaaaaaaaaaa

HE: What? What did I do?[6]

I rest my case.

---

6. Du-u-uh.

THREE

Lipsticks to Scrunchies:

Buy 'Em by the Barrel

W HEN IT COMES TO BUYING COSMETICS, girls learn at a very early age that there is great comfort to be gained from purchasing in large quantities. One thing that can be predicted with absolute certainty is that there is virtually no chance of a woman having just *one* lipstick tube or nail-polish bottle on her vanity table. This would be harder to find than Dennis Rodman's marriage license.

For some unexplained girl reason, we feel it

incumbent upon ourselves to purchase at least a dozen of the hot "hues du jour" featured on the display counters of drug and department stores. And on each subsequent visit we buy a half dozen more, until not only the tops of our dressers are completely covered with bottles and tubes, but the drawers are so jammed, it will take Roseanne's Thighmaster[1] to pry them open.

If we ever took all these lipsticks and placed them end to end, they would encircle the globe roughly twice. Men are always asking the pointless question, Why do we need to buy one thousand when just one or two would do? Well, du-u-uh. This overabundance happens for a very valid "girl-type" reason, mister. Unfortunately, women are the main targets of those clever fashion magazine ad campaigns designed by men who have Harvard Business School degrees and wear feather boas with their three-piece suits. So every month we open the pages to find yet another irresistable lipstick with "use me" names like "Sensual Satin" or "Pulsating Plum." Naturally, in the fashion magazines these shades are being worn by the sexiest lips on the planet, lips belonging to such totally hot babes as Halle Berry and Cindy Crawford.[2]

After we apply the "Pulsating Plum" and look into

---

1. Or Roseanne's actual thighs.

2. Cindy's lips have their own separate career and agent.

the mirror, we expect to see Halle Berry staring back with her moist lips glistening and quivering all over the place. Instead, what we see are lips the same color and texture as Mike Wallace's liver spots. "What is this?" we scream. Why does every perfectly gorgeous color in the lipstick tube turn into some grotesque shade when applied to our own lips?

Another common lipstick catastrophe occurs when our lipstick, painstakingly applied with a lipstick brush, ends up smeared across our front teeth. Even women with Ph.D.s have never been able to figure out how to avoid this. We certainly don't start out applying the lipstick directly to our teeth—although maybe we should, and save ourselves a step.

Then, it's not bad enough to look like your kid has finger-painted across your teeth, but now you've got to deal with all those irritating people who "subtly" point it out to you. They either silently point their fingers at their teeth, arching a haughty eyebrow as if to say, "My, my, don't we look dorky?" or else they commandeer the P.A. system at Kmart and announce it to all the shoppers. Yet, when somebody takes your picture at a public event, he never informs you of this problem. So the result is always horrifying: You're smiling a great big smile, with a mouth that looks as though you had just had your gums filleted at Benihana's.

We buy hundreds of different shades of nail polish with the same reckless abandon as we do lipsticks. In fact, most women have enough enamel on hand to paint a structure the size of Graceland. And nowadays we need extra coverage, because those acrylic nails we wear are as long as your average airport runway. It's also vitally important to have the shades that exactly match our lipsticks so we can achieve that perfectly coordinated look. And why is the "coordinated look" so important? Because the fashion magazines say it is. And if they say so, it automatically becomes gospel. Amen.[3]

And now that the latest trend is to wear nail-polish colors like blues, greens, and yellows in addition to the traditional reds and pinks, we have a lot more to purchase than ever before. I think it's accurate to say that most women have at least one dresser drawer designated for storing all two thousand shades that have been identified in the color spectrum—and a few that haven't.

As far as storing our collections goes, we all start out with good intentions. In the early stages, we invest a lot of money in clever nail-polish and lipstick caddies that neatly stack the items in easy-to-reach compartments. But after a few months of habitual buying, we need to increase our storage space tenfold. Then, after a

---

3. Fashion magazines have replaced Gideon Bibles in all major hotels.

while, the caddies don't satisfy our needs anymore. So we go on to larger containers, like wicker baskets and eventually OPEC oil drums. After a short time, even those aren't enough. We become addicts, hooked on a cosmetic habit that is spinning out of control faster than Gelsey Kirkland with a broken toe shoe. It would take a twelve-step program and painful withdrawal to part with even one of our bottles.

LET'S TURN OUR ATTENTION now to the "scrunchie." This is the third item in the trilogy of things we accumulate in numbers approaching infinity. Scrunchies are those cute little hair doodads, constructed basically by sewing a rag around a rubber band and then charging the same price for it as an ounce of pure gold. However, the function of scrunchies ranks up there in importance with brain surgery. This is because they rescue women from that most dreaded condition, "the bad-hair day." And since most females spend 99 percent of their lives enduring bad-hair days, these little items have become as necessary for the continuation of our species as mascara.

Just as with our lipstick and nail polish, we need a scrunchie to match every single piece of clothing in our wardrobe—not to mention our nighties and underwear. I store my collection in a huge wicker basket on my bedroom floor. But a strange thing keeps happening. Their numbers seem to be growing exponentially. I swear they must be asexually reproducing in the basket. We can only hope that Einstein was right when he said that the universe is constantly expanding, because judging from the numbers of scrunchies, we are going to need storage space measured in light-years.[4]

A matching scrunchie can do wonders to pull an outfit together and give a woman that totally coordinated look. Even though it takes me about the same time to put on my peach-colored suit and match it with peach lipstick, blusher, nail polish, shoes, and scrunchie as it took to build the Great Wall of China, the look is worth it. Of course, there are times when I enter a peach-colored room and seem to dematerialize into thin air like a crew member of the starship *Enterprise*. Whatever. I still think the look is way cool. So beam me up, Scottie.

---

4. Or one hell of a black hole.

FOUR

Women's Underwear:

A Brief History

S INCE THE BEGINNING OF TIME, women's underwear has been a fascinating and mystical subject. In
fact, it should be classified as one of the Seven
Other Wonders of the World. Even though the primary
reason for underwear has been to make a woman feel
comfortable, it's ironic that from day one it's been constructed in shapes and styles whose predominant purpose has been to inflict torture. If we dig back far
enough into history, we'd probably find that the first

corset was designed and distributed by the Marquis de Sade Catalogue.

It's really no mystery that Elizabeth I remained a virgin queen for seventy years. There was no man in the realm, including Merlin, who could get at her through that body corset made of chain mail and featuring spikes. The royal corset was obviously designed for battle, not the bedroom. Also, Elizabeth was in desperate need of two products, Rogaine and cheek blusher. But that's another story.

What was it with those body binders that pushed the breasts up so far they made contact with chin? Were women so unattractive that it was necessary to thrust a pair of bobbing boobs right under a man's nose to get his attention? It's a wonder that men back then were able to concentrate on anything else—like winning a war. And judging from the messed-up conditions of their countries, I guess they didn't.

It seems to me that these corsets worked at cross-purposes. While the breasts were relentlessly squeezed into their most voluptuous angle to attract men, their owners tended to pass out from lack of oxygen. This left precious little time for actually building a relationship or resolving issues. However, the men didn't notice anything unusual about the sex.

A few centuries later, women turned their attention

away from the bosom to the waist. The fad started during the Civil War era, with Southern women. They fanatically pursued the goal of attempting to truss their thirty-something-inch waists down to sixteen inches by tugging on corset strings made from the bootstraps of dead Yankees. This practice quickly spread to the North, where it became more popular than Patrick Swayze's dirty dancing at cotillions.

Because of these corsets, women remained as weak as kittens for the next hundred years. Is it really surprising that women didn't get any rights until after the 1900s? Owing to our own underwear, we remained pretty much unconscious for the first four centuries after Columbus.

Then for the next fifty years, breasts virtually disappeared off the face of the earth. They were bound (and maybe even gagged) or hidden under yards and yards of billowing cloth and shawls. During the Roaring Twenties, it was very much in vogue to be built like a boy and even more chic to drink like one. Breasts were out—and booze was in. The women of this era gave up the practice of enticing men by displaying their breasts on bras built like launching pads. They got smart and used vodka and black underpants instead.

Then, as the nation sobered up toward the 1950s, we once again focused our attention on the breast. This time it was Hollywood that was responsible for elevating the breast to its rightful place in history. Marilyn Monroe, Jayne Mansfield, Gina Lollobrigida, Anita Ekberg, Diana Dors, and Jane Russell collectively possessed more mammary tissue than the rest of the world's population combined. And the great inventors of that era spent a lot of their spare time designing bras that would transform even a AAA-cup figure into a bulging, pulsating mass of D-cup illusion.

If the truth were known, Howard Hughes's greatest accomplishment was not his plane, the Spruce Goose. It was actually the "aerodynamic bra" design he did for Jane Russell for her film debut in *The Outlaw*. It provided the "lift" necessary to get those huge "propellers" off her stomach.

Another very popular foundation garment of the fifties was the Merry Widow. It was strapless and was constructed from state-of-the-art materials of the day: Tupperware and Formica. These bras were practically indestructible and reputedly survived the first A-bomb test in Alamogordo. The Merry Widow was so intractable that even while its wearer was doing a vigorous cha-cha at the prom, the cups always pointed straight ahead while the rest of the body twisted and turned with the music.[1] They were also made with

1. Boy Scouts used it to set "true north" on their compasses.

approximately seventy-five hooks up the back, which required advanced manual dexterity to unhook. Parents of teenage girls all over America encouraged them to wear Merry Widows on all their dates because unless the guy was David Copperfield, there was no way he was ever going to get to first base with their daughters.

One of the most popular bras back then was the "bullet bra." These bras were named for the shape your breast took on after being squeezed into cups that were stitched with five hundred concentric circles of belted steel thread. They actually squeezed each breast into a point sharper than your average number two pencil. Like the Merry Widow, these bras were also so sturdily constructed that the only maintenance they needed was to be brought into the tire shop for an annual retread.

The precursor of our modern Wonder Bra was also designed back in the fifties; it was called the "push-up" bra. It captured every mammary cell on a woman's chest and forced them into one big bulge that peeked out over the tops of those famous fifties peasant blouses. They could create cleavage on anyone, including Milton Berle. The only downside was that in the rare event a guy managed to unfasten one of these bras, he was in for the disappointment of his life when he discovered that all that lovely cleavage was merely an optical illusion. Sadly, he was left to gaze upon a chest that had about the same sex appeal as his eight-year-old brother's.

One of the major forces of the fifties' undercover industry was Frederick's of Hollywood. Frederick's sexy catalogue was found under more teenage boys' beds than wads of gum. They showed page after page of tantalizing bras, girdles, garter belts, and inventive cut-out lingerie worn by models drawn with more curves than Mulholland Drive. Among the most popular item of the time was the "French Cut-out" bra. Frederick made millions when he snipped the ends off bra cups and exploited the nipple to get that stand-at-attention silhouette under clingy sweaters. Anyway, you must remember that the nipple was a rare anatomical find in the fifties. But if you wore the bra in temperatures under thirty-two degrees Fahrenheit, it made your nipples look about the size of Texas.[2]

Long before breast implants came on the scene, women were surreptitiously ordering "falsies" from the small ads in the backs of magazines. They were made of the same foam rubber as your sofa cushions and could double as shock absorbers.

Even though we were heavily into the breast thing in the fifties, girdles ruled. And the fifties girdle was

2. And brought record numbers of lawsuits involving frostbite.

brought to you by the same folks who manufactured tires in Akron, Ohio. Made from crude neoprene, these garments were built to withstand 15,000 pounds of pressure per square inch of packed female cellulite.

It was not uncommon to hear about women who underwent a spontaneous blowout on the dance floor while executing those dangerous dips while swing-dancing. The rubber girdle stretched from the ribs and down to the thighs, and every inch of flesh was virtually vacuum-packed by the pressure the girdle exerted. These casings also had removable metal fasteners clipped to the bottom of each leg, which held up our nylons. And these miserable things dug so deep into the skin that over the years they broke all the blood vessels in your upper leg. In fact, you could actually tell a woman's age by counting the rings of broken veins around her thighs.

To get these girdles off you practically required the Jaws of Life. This is why there were almost no teenage pregnancies in the fifties. Very few guys possessed the kind of strength it took to peel one of these girdles off a gal.

Looking back, it's not surprising that we were an incredibly humorless nation. Our chosen leaders, like Richard Nixon and Joe McCarthy, never provided the kind of political entertainment we've had with Clinton. But even if they could, our women were in such peril from their strangulating underwear that a hearty laugh could have dislocated a kidney. So we suffered in silence for more than a decade, until once again, history repeated itself and our fascination with hips, breasts, and bras went out of style during the 1970s.

Women actually took to burning their bras in protest. And for a time there, we were protesting just about everything—Vietnam, inequality, tainted tunafish, shaving our legs, lack of jobs, lack of orgasms—you name it. We were so angry that we burned enough bras in a year to heat the state of North Dakota.

Then, in the late seventies, a curious thing happened. David Bowie appeared on stage in a strapless bra covered with ostrich feathers and rhinestones. And it was so flattering, the bra came back into fashion with a vengeance.[3]

The 1980s ushered in an era of women's rights, freedom, and personal choice. Suddenly, "braless" became our national alternative dress code. However, large-breasted women encountered serious problems trying to keep their breasts off their knees for most of this era.

This problem was solved in the nineties, when duct tape technically became classified as underwear. Women discovered that if they just placed a strip under each breast

---

3. George Michael is doing the same thing for the millennium.

and extended it around their ribs, they had instant support, cleavage, and the potential for installing an entire cooling system under their clothes. Besides on your ceilings and under your sink, duct tape was now found under strapless gowns, sheer blouses, and even bathing suits. It was like a miracle drug with no side effects and offered more support than A.A.

When a company called Victoria's Secret was founded, it knocked Frederick's out of Hollywood and just about every other place in America. They kicked some serious butt by introducing a line of incredibly sexy bras, thong panties, and negligees. Then they marketed their line, using a collection of the most voluptuous models ever genetically engineered. In fact, many of the models' breasts are so large, they have their own zip codes.

The models are seen not only posed erotically in the Victoria's Secret catalogue but also in TV commercials and on the Internet. Women love shopping for sexy, feminine lingerie, and their men love seeing them in it. A man is free to drool over the girls in the catalogue or in their stores *and still* make his woman happy by buying her some delicious, silky item. Now that's one smart company.

The other item that Victoria's Secret brought to our culture was the thong panty. This little piece of silk is merely a G-string adapted for use off the stage. And do they ever command big bucks for a piece of cloth that offers less coverage than one of Ed McMahon's insurance policies.

Personally, I hate the idea of a thong. For Pete's sake, I've spent my whole life pulling my underwear out of there! Besides, they are not only uncomfortable but also potentially dangerous. They have been known to give a woman an episiotomy while she was doing a deep-knee bend in the gym. It's pretty apparent these obsessions with our breasts, hips, and thighs has made life very difficult for us girls. It would be a lot easier if we just did what guys do and turned our underwear inside out when we needed a new pair.

FIVE

Feminine Hygiene Products:

The Personals

I USED TO THINK that I was a fairly well groomed
woman and certainly not offensive to the population at large. But that was before I became enlight-
ened by all the magazine and TV ads warning women
that every time we move, speak, or cross our legs, we're

felling thousands of innocent bystanders with our toxic body odors. Frankly, there aren't enough hours in the day for us to use all the feminine hygiene products they say we need.

In light of all this "hygiene hype," we have to ask ourselves two tough questions:

1. Is it necessary to have a separate deodorant spray for every orifice of our body?
2. If we didn't use these products, would women really smell like dead mackerel?

I admit I've been thoroughly brainwashed by buying into all this hype. In fact, I have to allow from 7 A.M. until noon every day to accommodate my daily feminine hygiene routine. And before I actually get into bed every night, I'm feminizing until well past midnight. But herein lies the rub. The prep time it takes to become the cleanest, freshest, most germ-free, and most desirable woman on the planet leaves no time for my sex life. Go figure.

Anyhow, I begin my ritual with a forty-five-minute shower and a checklist of the items I'll need to use. My shower stall is so filled with products, it looks like a Y2K survival shelter. But I need to use all of them to follow the rules set forth by the high priestesses of hygiene.

First of all, you can't wash with just plain soap anymore. Nowadays you have to use the specially formulated antibacterial, antifungal, antiperspirant shower gel applied with a buff-puff. Then you must loofah yourself in order to exfoliate all those unattractive dead cells, which have reputedly been keeping you from total fulfillment as a woman.

After loofahing comes the all-important shave, skillfully executed with a state-of-the-art razor blade. It costs $49.95, but that's because it has been "scientifically engineered" for women[1] to get at those "hard-to-reach" parts. Proceed with caution. You'll be venturing into shaving territory virtually uncharted by the Gillette people.

It's funny, but I remember back in the Dark Ages, when I was in high school, it was perfectly okay to shave your legs only to the knee. In the sixties, you weren't considered hip unless your armpit hair was long enough to braid. But by today's standards, even some light down on the thigh is considered unhygienic and butch.

The millennium body must be shaved all the way up both thighs, around the backs of the legs, around the bikini area, under the arms, on the tops of the toes and in any other spot suspect of harboring a renegade follicle.

---

1. It has a pink rubber grip.

The number one problem of being hairless, besides shivering like a Chihuahua, is that your cellulite can no longer lie camouflaged by peach fuzz. Now those dreaded lumps and bumps are just "out there," looking a lot like moguls on a ski trail. Therefore, a nation of desperate women demanded that the cosmetic companies come up with a product that gets rid of cellulite without liposuction or other surgeries.

One company did market a cellulite cream that claims to break up cellulite deposits under the skin and redistribute them around the body more evenly. This is supposedly accomplished by a combination of applying the anticellulite cream and then mushing it in with a contraption that looks like a rubber rolling pin. But you have to do it with so much force that though you might squash the lumps, you'll raise bruises the size of an adult liver.

At some point during my toilette, I start thinking about those dumb feminine hygiene commercials on TV. As far as I'm concerned, they are more offensive than my body odor could ever be.

The most memorable one is where the mother and daughter are discussing their most personal hygiene problems while standing in the middle of a line of forty people at Starbucks. The mother is telling the daughter that she's not as clean and fresh as she thinks, then punctuates her point by pulling a huge bottle of Massengill out of her Fendi tote bag. The daughter then spills her double latte nonfat mocha frappuccino while trying to crawl under the table. That remark shows the kind of deep love and unmitigated chutzpah only a mother could deliver.

Many women feel it incumbent on themselves to tack on another fifteen minutes to the daily regimen and go for the douche du jour. However, douching can upset the natural moisture balance of a woman's delicate tissues. At least that's what I hear on the six o'clock news as reported by Dan Rather. So in order to counteract this fact, I have to use one of those moisture replacement products so I can walk a few feet without suffering friction burns.

After I've cleansed, shaved, exfoliated, douched, degermed, and deodorized every square millimeter of my body, now it has to be moisturized. This takes several applications of aloe vera gel, anticellulite cream, and collagen-boosting lotions. This is followed by a healthy dusting with powder to keep the moisture trapped in the skin. But you cannot use just an ordinary garden variety of talcum powder. God forbid. It *has* to be the antibacterial kind fortified with hexachlorophene, trimethylchloride, soybean oil, lysergic acid diethylamide, and Lysol.

The final step before I get dressed is to spray every orifice on my body with a different aerosol, each specially formulated for "problem areas." And judging from the number of spray cans I need, it's obvious that I've got more problem areas than Iraq. But I dutifully spray every one of them because, God forbid, I wouldn't want to take a chance on offending anybody out there, including the guys in my gym who have been pumping iron since dawn.

One of the most important choices in the hygiene lottery is the right underarm deodorant. The TV ads dramatize thousands of men and women who are publicly humiliated after raising their arms and revealing sweat stains the size of Lake Superior. It's mandatory that our deodorant contain an antiperspirant to prevent this from happening.

A secondary, but no less embarrassing, problem is also documented in the ads. It shows a woman in a sleeveless blouse waving to her kids, when the cameras zero in on some chalky deodorant residue that looks like she took a caulking gun to her armpits. This look did not win her any awards.[2] So caveat emptor, carpe diem, and cut the crap. Choose carefully. The roll-ons can be gummy, the gels can be sticky, and the glide-ons can be waxy. I prefer a spray

---

2. However, the commercial is up for a Clio.

deodorant because I hate feeling like I've spread mayonnaise under my armpits.

When I'm finally ready to get dressed, I have to remind myself to use a pantiliner before I step into my underpants. Could any woman afford to pass up that "oh so fresh" feeling? And I'd better use the ones with "wings," because by now I'm so late, I'll need them to get to wherever I'm going really fast. I also stick a pair of Odor-Eaters under my arms, as well as in my shoes, for extra protection. At this point, I am so full of shields, I could go out on the street and take a round of gunfire.

Before applying my makeup, I scrutinize my face in a magnifying mirror, searching for clogged pores. We used to call them blackheads in the old days, but you can't anymore—it's just too politically incorrect. And back then, one of your mother's cardinal rules was that you were never supposed to squeeze these ugly little things. You had to put your face over a bowl of boiling water to steam them out. I don't know if they thought that the blackheads would simply fall into the bowl of boiling water by themselves or what. But it did wonders to clear up your sinuses.

Recently, they have made pore cleansing a lot easier with the invention of little Band-Aid–shaped "strips." You simply apply them over the clogged pores, wait fifteen minutes, and then pull them off. They contain some active ingredient that draws the dirt out of the pores and makes it adhere to the strip. It works really well, and it's very addicting to check out all the various patterns left behind on the adhesive.

THANK HEAVENS I AM THROUGH MENOPAUSE and don't have to worry about tampons and sanitary pads any longer. In fact, the memories are so bad, I don't even want to go there. Instead, now it's my bladder that's giving me the problems. I am falling victim to having the occasional "oops moment"—when I laugh too loud or make a hard landing when exiting my RV.[3]

3. Its height is approximately the same as that of a 747.

Self-help Groups:
Support Can Be Beautiful

ABOUT THE ONLY THING men fear more than talking about their emotions is being dragged to a bridal shower. On the rare occasions when they do get together for male bonding, the conversation never gets more personal than what size nail it takes to hammer a two-by-four to the wall. But women—that's another story. We were created with an enormous need to act as one another's psychiatrists, counselors, and confessors. This probably accounts for why we are so much better adjusted than men.[1]

There's no subject too personal, too inflammatory, or too embarrassing for women to discuss. We make it a priority to "be there" for each other anytime of the day or night to give each other comfort and emotional support. This is strongly evidenced by the fact that we never go to the ladies' room without a support group.

But like everything else in today's society, this uniquely female trait has been exploited to make money. Our original concept has mutated into that hideous entity we commonly refer to as the "support group." There's one out there for just about every condition that ails us. There are groups for people who are too fat, too thin, too violent, too passive, drink too much, smoke too much, and gamble too much. There's even one for people who have too much sex—if that's possible. This one is especially helpful for those who crave doing it with people they're not married to.

There are also groups for obsessive-compulsives, anal-retentives, passive-aggressives, and a host of other illnesses recognizable by the hyphen in the name. And with the stresses placed on women by our modern society, we need a lot of help to cope. In fact, most of

---

1. The Gospel . . . according to women.

us belong to so many of these groups, we can't go out in public without being recognized.

I strongly believe that when we move beyond our "kaffeeklatsch" therapy and join one of these support groups, we are sabotaging ourselves. The psychobabble alone that you're exposed to at these meetings is enough to drive you into another support group.

In the old days, no one had "issues"—we had problems. If you got dumped by your boyfriend, then you had a problem. But now it's an "issue," and what's worse, it's an issue that has no "closure." It's politically incorrect to call the guy a "big jerk"—now he's "emotionally unavailable." The group will undoubtedly say that you didn't really get dumped for another woman, but instead, it was a case of his needing to "explore his sexuality." And even though the bum only took you out one night a week because he was out getting loaded the other six, the group will say that you didn't make it "quality time."

I might be crazy, but I think that we'd be a lot better off handling our problems the way we used to. In the old days when a girlfriend and her beer-guzzling boyfriend broke up, it was a major cause for girl-rallying. All the enraged gal-pals showed up at the grieving girlfriend's house to lend their support. They spent hours cursing him out, sticking pins through his picture, and in general, trashing him so badly that Charlie Sheen looked like a saint in comparison.

After the girls had a good six-hanky cry together, the deserted girlfriend felt relief and gained the confidence to move ahead with her life. And God forbid the ex-boyfriend should show up at her doorstep to try to talk things over. He'd be walking into an environment more hostile than the Lilith Fair, and the women would turn on him like a pack of female wolves with PMS.

Another problem with support groups is that they usually lead to getting addicted to other support groups. For example, I had a girlfriend who was in a destructive relationship and went to one of these support groups for a year. And during that year, the only significant thing that happened was, she got addicted to coffee and cigarettes. So then she had to join a smoke-enders support group. This group's therapy consisted of being subjected to hours of movies showing people with holes in their throats and voices like Harvey Fierstein's. After a month, she was so desperate to get away from the group, she actually quit cold turkey all by herself.

There's a reason why support groups are such a thriving business. And that's because it's human nature to replace one compulsion with another. This was true of my friend. After successfully kicking a two-pack-a-day habit, she replaced it with a two-pound-a-day M&M

habit. Then after gaining forty pounds in one year, she figured she'd better join Overeaters Anonymous.

In this group she found herself surrounded by hundreds of women all struggling to regain their self-esteem and their former dress sizes. There were tales of late-night Oreo binges and lost weekends with Ben and Jerry. These were counteracted by pep talks, weigh-ins, and guest speakers giving inspirational talks about their own weight-loss successes. It took her about six months to lose all her extra weight. But I honestly don't believe she got her motivation from the therapy group. I think that her prime motivation was the very real fear that Richard Simmons might appear on her doorstep one day with a camera crew.

Whatever her motivation, she ended up looking great. She joined a gym, started working out, and toned her body up like a Barbie doll. Unfortunately, it was Steroid Barbie. She had a short-term problem with those, too. In spite of it, she became a knockout[2] and never lacked for men at her doorstep.[3] She also collected a stable of guys who wined and dined her every night of the week. But after a year—you got it—she became hopelessly addicted to sex.

---

2. In her pumped-up condition, she could deliver one, too.

3. Encyclopedia salesmen, Mormons, and Jehovah's Witnesses.

Then she had to decide whether she needed to join a support group for this new addiction. After taking a confidential, scientific sex test from one of those expert magazines,[4] she decided that she did need help. This decision was based on the fact that she answered yes to all ten of the following questions:

1. Do you often appear at the door wrapped in plastic like your grandmother's couch?
2. Do you attend family reunions to meet guys?
3. Do you own sex toys that require a Die Hard battery to operate?
4. If your boyfriend complained that you should act more interested in his family, would you sleep with his brother?
5. When you get intellectually turned on, does your brain get as hard as a rock?
6. Do you employ anyone for domestic work referred to as "Cabana Boy"?
7. Are your boyfriends so young that when the relationship is over you consider adopting them?
8. Do you often use sex enhancers like Viagra nasal spray? Is sneezing more fun?
9. Have you gone from trying to get multiple orgasms to trying to get rid of multiple organisms?

---

4. *Cosmo.*

10. Growing up, was your favorite doll Dominatrix Barbie?

My friend said that the women in the sex-addicted support group were in much worse shape than those who tried to kick cigarettes cold turkey. There's nothing meaner or more dangerous than a bunch of horny women. Their therapy consisted of trying to find more positive ways of channeling their sexual energy and emotional neediness into more productive activities.

So . . . at the completion of the four-month program, the members had knitted enough scarves to clothe the Bosnian army and performed enough community service to get out of jail free for the next twenty years. My friend also developed a brand-new skill. She learned to become one hell of a cardplayer. Poker, bridge, blackjack, you name it—she mastered it. And, yep. She became totally hooked on gambling.

This new addiction led to a brief stint in Gamblers Anonymous and hundreds of comped rooms at Caesars Palace. But she wisely chose the former and with the help of G.A. kicked the habit in less than a year. She also met a wonderful, supportive man in the group and married him a short time later. They lived happily ever after—for about a year, until she came home one day and found him wearing her bra, panties, and garter belt.

Frantically, she scanned the Yellow Pages in search of support groups for the spouses of transvestites. But she couldn't find any. So one morning at 3 A.M. when she was at the end of her rope, she called me up. I immediately corralled about ten other girlfriends and we arrived at her house carrying placards with slogans like BURN HIS THONG and STRANGLE HIM WITH HIS GARTER BELT. We were outraged. We were livid. We were all suffering from PMS . . . and you know the rest of the story. Trust me, it wasn't pretty.

SEVEN

Price Club/Costco:

Going for Broke

WHEN YOU SHOP AT A PLACE THAT PROVIDES FLATBEDS alongside its supersized grocery carts, you know you're in trouble. You've got to figure you'll be dropping some serious simoleons even though your game plan is just to pick up a "few items." These warehouse "price clubs," like Costco, Sam's Club, and B.J.'s, can be either shoppers' paradise or shoppers' hell. This is because the kind of shopping you do there requires something similar to basic training. You'll need to be both physically and mentally fit to fight the crowds at warehouse clubs.

First of all, these places are as big as Arizona and even hotter in the summer. Likewise, you'll freeze in the winter because, God forbid, they have to spend a cent extra on anything as frivolous as heat. I have learned from experience that in order to survive a Costco or Sam's Club, there are two things you need to do:

1. Before you go there to shop, work out with a personal trainer for at least a month.
2. When you're through shopping, apply for a second mortgage.

There's no way you can leave one of these stores without writing a check for at least six hundred bucks or more. The problem is that they have thousands of items on the shelves that call out to you like the Sirens in the *Odyssey.* For example, take the "deluxe vegetable steamer." After you see it, you wonder how you ever made it through your life without it. This is how the subtle addiction begins. And men are not immune to it, either. They have weaknesses every bit as bad as women's. They get sucked in by items that call out to them like the naked women in *Sirens.* Men are rendered powerless at the sight of camcorders, barbecue grills, and radial tires. And when they see the display of camping gear and kayaks, you've lost them. You've also just lost about five hundred bucks.

My husband and I go on these Costco binges about once a month. He immediately steers the cart to the junk-food aisle and resides in hog heaven loading up on the beef jerky. How anyone can eat this stuff[1] is beyond me. It looks like cadaver muscles. Besides, jerky isn't exactly cheap. It runs about six or seven dollars a package. However, my husband insists that jerky is one of the major food groups, along with Chee-tos and Coors.

You can spot the personal-hygiene products area by the mob of cranky women grabbing tampons sold in boxes of five hundred. No wonder they're all in a bad mood. Any woman who needs this many pads also needs a D and C. After we load up on toothpaste, shampoo, and enough deodorant to make even the Steelers' locker room smell good, my husband reluctantly trades in our overloaded shopping cart for one of those flatbed things.

Once you hit the frozen-food section, it's a major traffic jam. Women are ruthlessly broadsiding each other with their shopping cards, vying for a position closer to the freezer units. Just about any frozen food you can think of is stocked and packaged in quantities that would feed the entire Osmond family.

---

1. Doesn't actually qualify as food.

And even though there are only two of you, how could you pass up the frozen pasta primavera packaged in six-cubic-foot pans? So throw another shrimp on the barbie. When you load up on the twenty-pound bags of shelled, deveined shrimp, you'll break into a chorus of "Waltzing Matilda." Plus, there are bags of one hundred deboned, skinless chicken breasts and enough frozen lasagna to feed Venice. Greed is good. The only thing left to do is rationalize why it's a good idea to buy this much food.

That's when you come up with the idea of throwing several dinner parties. And why not? Right at your fingertips are sushi on trays, salsa in tubs, wine in crates, and cheesecakes so large, they can be seen from the space shuttle *Discovery*. The party section offers matching paper plates, cups, tablecloths, and even plastic wineglasses.

At this point, your husband has broken out in hives and is urging you to finish ASAP. But as you're heading toward the pharmacy to get him some Benadryl, you spot the aisle filled with cleaning products and remember that's what you came for in the first place. You can't help but feel some major guilt as your husband, who by now looks like he has cowpox, lifts the economy-size barrels of detergent, floor cleaner, and fabric softener onto the flatbed.

I guess it just isn't his day, because the silk-plant section is smartly placed just before the registers. This is yet another brilliant marketing strategy from the people who have elevated suckering shoppers to an art form. They know that once a woman eyeballs it, there's no way she's leaving without that seven-foot silk ficus in a pot covered with fake moss. Besides, think of all the fun your cat is going to have climbing it and scratching all the moss out of the pot.

In order to haul the ficus away, your husband has to go back to the entrance for a second flatbed. You're also totally clueless about how you're going to fit this seven-foot mon-strosity into your car. But at this point, you wouldn't care if you had to tie it to the roof like a Christmas tree, because there's no way you're leaving the lot without it.

Finally, you're ready to check out. That's when you realize that the shortest line is longer than the one at the premiere of the latest *Star Wars* movie. And while you're standing there for close to an hour, you just hap-pen to remember a "couple of items" you forgot to get. So you leave your husband guarding the haul and start running back down the aisles.

Your husband is looking very peaked and nervous by now. In fact, he's sweating more than you do during a hot flash. So you frantically run around loading up with at least another hundred bucks' worth of stuff. By the time you get to the checkout, your husband's pallor is so scary you have to put a mirror under his nose to see if he's still breathing. As he watches the tally mount up on the register, he grabs a large grocery sack and starts hyperventilating into it. When the grand total appears, he clutches his heart and staggers as though he's about to faint. He's in good company, though. Fainting is such a common occurrence at the checkout registers, they have medical personnel with wheelchairs waiting to catch all the husbands on their way down.

Trying to load up your car is a strategically important task in itself. You'll need plenty of rope and bungee cords to secure all your purchases in or on any part of your vehicle. It's not uncommon to see vehicles exiting the parking lot with spouses bungeed to the hood or roof. After you get home, you swear you'll never step foot in that place again.

But then you think about the bargains and realize that before long it will be Christmas. And you know what that means—fighting nightmare crowds of shoppers whose idea of being filled with the holiday spirit is to get all liquored up. And there's absolutely no question that they'll kill for the last fruitcake left on the shelves. So you'd better come early and you'd better come armed. 'Tis the season.

EIGHT

Implants:

Replacement Parts

FEEL DEPRESSED? Get a lift—literally. You may choose from any one of a number of implants available on the market. In today's world, it's as common as getting a high colonic. Some of the options in implants are dental, breast, cheek, or chin. There are also synthetic materials like Gore-Tex that a surgeon can implant into deep facial lines or in the lips to plump them out. And unlike fat or collagen, Gore-Tex won't be absorbed by the body. Just look to your old Fila ski pants from the eighties for proof.

Besides cosmetic implants, you can have metal replacement parts implanted, like pacemakers, which regulate the heartbeat, or electric stimulators to relieve pain. And these parts can last forever.[1] It's becoming so common now that there are people walking around with 50 percent of their bodies composed of man-made materials. So the question becomes: How much synthetic material can we put into our breasts and other body parts before we are officially declared another life form, like an android?

It seems to me that the ones who benefit most from implants are the doctors. They're making a fortune from them. It's not surprising, because it's been prophesied in the scriptures for thousands of years: you reap what you sow. After these doctors plant a little piece of plastic or silicone in the body, they sit back and reap megabucks. America's biggest bumper crop of the new millennium will be boobs. There are no age barriers, either. Women are having breast implants done as young as eighteen and well into their seventies. I can't tell you how many sixty-year-old women I know who have six-month-old breasts. But here's the thing. What's going to happen to

---

1. Or until the warranty runs out.

all the eighteen-year-olds in a few years when they get pregnant? The combined D-cup implants plus all the natural expanding tissue will make their breasts so humongous, they'll be forced to wear their maternity clothes upside down.

I don't have anything against women getting implants. What does bother me, though, is that there is a certain level of dishonesty among many of them who get this procedure done. First of all, none of them ever admits that the main reason they're doing it is to get guys to look at them. They always recite the same rhetoric: "I'm doing it to please myself." Oh, sure you are.

So why is it that you'll never see a woman who just had implants keeping her boobs under wraps in a J. Crew button-down blouse? No way. They always choose to debut them in a spandex number revealing so much breast, you can practically read the Dow-Corning label on them. Gimme a break. Most of them end up with boobs so huge they need a building permit for them. Then when they parade by some unsuspecting construction workers with their boobs jiggling like crazy under a teeny-tiny low-cut tank top, and the guys make a remark,[2] they act all offended and everything.

This is exactly why guys always insist that women are

---

2. Accompanied by sucking noises and animal grunts.

all screwed up and don't know what they really want. Even the Spice Girls, in their infinite wisdom,[3] have recognized this. And in this case, I'd have to agree with the men.[4] It's definitely a case of the mixed message raised to an art form. I don't know why women just can't be honest about it. What's wrong with saying that we want big boobs so guys will think we look sexy? What's the big deal about admitting that?

I once appeared on a TV talk show with a stripper named Chesty Love, whose claim to fame was her 115-inch bust. She got to be that big by finding a doctor who injected her implants with saline[5] over a number of years. They weighed about thirty pounds and she had to wear a special bra 24/7 to support them. But they actually ended up supporting her, because she was able to command ten times her former stripping fee. Then she battled the IRS and got them to let her declare her breasts as stage props so she could take an annual tax deduction on them. Now this is not only a smart woman, but an honest one. The only smarter move she could have made would be to declare them as a small country and collect property taxes.

---

3. Combined IQ of 58.

4. An occurrence as frequent as Halley's comet.

5. Same number of gallons as the Red Sea.

Besides big breasts, many women also have a thing for big cheekbones. Really big ones. As in the kind that make them look like Jack Palance. In keeping with this look, many also want to have chin implants done. I remember when Carol Burnett had her chin remodeled. Like everybody else on the planet, I tuned in to see what she looked like. Most of us sat there breathless during her traditional Tarzan call to see if the implant would move around and end up on her neck someplace. It didn't.

Dental implants have become popular in the last ten years too. However, they are very expensive and it's very time-consuming to have them put in. Dental implants are, basically, fake teeth that are permanently screwed into the jawbone. They are often done on people who have lost their teeth to periodontal problems. The only downside is that the ones with significant bone loss from this disease often come out resembling Morton Downey, Jr. All those fake ivories look like a pianist could play Beethoven's Seventh in your mouth.

Another really remarkable thing is how surgeons implant synthetic material like Gore-Tex to fill out deep facial lines and furrows. The Gore-Tex looks like a plump spongy piece of yarn, which is inserted in one end of the deep line and actually pulled out through the opposite end. This is often used in the naso-labial folds on either side of the nose, to restore a youthful appearance. It's also used above the bridge of the nose to puff out frown lines. And since Gore-Tex doesn't react with normal tissue, the only side effect would be if the string popped and made a big knot on your cheek, like Khrushchev's wen.

Gore-Tex is also implanted in the lips to make them puffy. It's for women who want the really sensuous, full-lipped look like Kelly LeBrock's.[6] Personally, I don't want to look like that. If I were a guy, I'd be scared of kissing lips that big and spongy. They look like they could suck in Cleveland. I'd be terrified that lips that huge would suck my brains out and leave me like a zombie, obeying every order a woman gave me. Wait a minute. This happens all the time, anyway—even without the Gore-Tex lips.

So there's nothing to fear about growing old anymore. The good news is that you can get a pacemaker to correct an irregular heartbeat, get plastic hips for crippling joint problems, or permanent teeth instead of dentures. You can also have electrical stimulators implanted for conditions like chronic back pain. Someday in the near future, people are going to be 80 percent synthetic, and the government will disqualify them for social security.

---

6. Or Mick Jagger.

NINE

Health Foods:

Eat, Drink, and Stay Hungry

WELL, IT TOOK ME LONG ENOUGH, but I finally got into the whole "healthy eating" thing. It was prompted by your typical middle-aged neurotic obsession with illness. After fifty, many of our friends are finally paying the price for smoking, hard drinking, and other vices that kept them in a good mood for decades. Forget romantic dinners. Forget preoccupation with sex. After the half-century mark, married couples go from being lovers to friends, and then end up as each other's nursemaids.

Lately, in my own home, our dinner conversations are consumed with descriptions of acid reflux, joint pain, and the state of our bowels. Even when we're having dinner with friends at an elegant restaurant, the conversation always deteriorates into kvetching sessions where we all compare our various symptoms, give advice on how to stay regular, and swap medical horror stories.

How did we get to this place from the carefree days of caffeine and corn dogs, three hours of sleep, and tequila shooters on Saturday night? We got here because if we didn't change some of our bad habits by forty or fifty years old, we were slated to live out the rest of our days in the ICU.

I decided to get into a more healthy lifestyle when my husband was diagnosed with Crohn's disease. Crohn's is a chronic inflammation of the large intestine. It can also involve the small intestine and the stomach. Many people with Crohn's also suffer from acid reflux, which is the backup of stomach acid, causing constant irritation to the esophageal lining. But what they do to you in order to diagnose this condition is almost worse than the disease itself.

My husband was hospitalized as an outpatient, where he had an endoscopy and colonoscopy done at the same time! After fifty, you can pretty much count on the fact that every medical exam they give you will involve a six-foot tube with a light attached to the end of it, used to probe any available orifice. Not only did my poor husband have the tube snaked down his esophagus, but also his entire small and large intestines were probed from the other end—and I'm not talking about the examination table, either.

However, diagnosing the problem is only the first step. Next, you've got to figure out how to treat it. The doctors gave my husband a truckload of pills to keep his symptoms under control. But in the long run, I felt he needed to make permanent changes in his diet to reverse the condition. So I started wearing the hats of doctor, nutritionist, therapist, and dietician. I figured I could not only help him but also treat my own critical problems— menopause, hot flashes, and cellulite. To do this, we needed to radically change the kinds of foods we were eating.

I got sucked into the whole nutritional healing movement when I began reading books by experts like Dr. Andrew Weil, who wrote *Live Long and Feel Good*. After reading how bad our American diets are, you'll wonder how you can still be walking around on your own steam and not hooked up to an I.V. drip. One thing Dr. Weil stresses is the importance of eating organic foods. These are foods that are grown without chemicals or pesticides. He also recommends eating certain foods you just can't get at your local grocery store, unless the store happens to be located in Japan. So I started going to one of the rapidly growing organic grocery stores called Whole Foods.

Going to Whole Foods is like entering a time tunnel and coming out in the 1960s. We're talking "natural" big time here. I quickly realized that Birkenstocks and braids[1] were the de rigueur attire for that place. The clientele looks like they just drove in from a commune after an entire morning of intently watching soil on the gardening channel. I believe the term "sprout-head" says it all. The first thing you notice when you walk through the doors is that this place has a distinct aroma. In fact, it smells a lot like your grandmother's root cellar. The first two aisles are devoted entirely to vitamins, supplements, herbs, and just about any type of holistic health aid you can think of. The shelves are lined with bottles of pills with names like bioflavenoids, chelated calcium, chromium picolinate, chondroitin, pycogenol, and a host of other substances that only a diction coach could pronounce correctly. It's anybody's guess whether these products will make you healthier, but you'll definitely become one hell of a Scrabble player.

---

1. Armpit hair.

Next comes the tea aisle, where you find exotic herbs like alfalfa, kukicha, dandelion, kava-kava, kombuscha, and astragalus. Then they have a whole section of teas devoted solely to alleviating female problems. Here you find brands with names like Female Sage, Mother's Milk, Pregnancy Tea, PMS Tea, and Good Mood Tea. It's impressive, although stocking the PMS Tea next to the Good Mood Tea seems like an oxymoron to me.

Next you move on to a huge vegetable section with signs indicating whether the vegetables are organically or conventionally grown. I don't need to read the signs, because I can tell just by looking at the price. A bag of conventionally grown tomatoes is two dollars, but the same bag of tomatoes organically grown without pesticides, fertilized by alfalfa-fed cow dung, nourished with purified water in an environment of controlled lighting and humidity will cost about the same as a pair of scalped tickets to a Streisand concert.

The veggie section offers items that heretofore you thought were only consumed by livestock. Among them, you'll see strange names like dinosaur black kale, bok choy, chard, jimaca, burdock root, daikon, and black kohash. This stuff looks like it should be available only on the black market. It also looks like you need to eat it with a roach clip.

One of the most "in" things they offer is wheatgrass juice. They grow the plants in a flat that reminds me of the kind of flats people living in apartments grow grass in for their cats. The greens "specialist" cuts it and stuffs it into a juicer, which compresses all the dark-green juice out of the grass. It's collected in a small one- or two-ounce cup. Now, let me warn you. This stuff is gamey! Remember, it's the same vegetation that sheep graze on.

The sissies mix it with carrot juice, but the truly macho drink it down straight like Rocky takes his raw eggs. Once you toss it back, you'll react like you just downed a shot of 150 proof moonshine—your body will give an involuntary shudder and you'll shout, "Mercy!" But the people who drink it religiously say it's really a trip.[2] It's actually touted as the perfect food.[3] I have no idea what's in it or what benefits it offers, but they'd better be pretty damn spectacular if I'm going to be swallowing this stuff every day.

Besides a great fish department, they also have foods that have been, up until now, eaten exclusively *by* fish. You can purchase packages of spirulina, chlorella, plankton, tamari, and more. They offer everything but night crawlers—which will probably be added any day now.

---

2. With marmalade hills and tangerine skies.

3. By discrimination ungulates everywhere.

Once you get your food home, you have to prepare it correctly. If the purists had their way, you would be eating everything raw. But that's not for me. After eating a steady diet of raw broccoli and cauliflower, you'll be emitting more gaseous fumes than a New York City transit bus. And news flash! You aren't supposed to microwave food anymore. This is anathema. They claim that it scrambles all the molecules, rendering the food more impotent than Bob Dole.

After six months, our health has improved significantly. The only problem is that we are starving. This food doesn't stick to your ribs[4] like a good steak. Ten minutes after "dinner," we are ravenous again. Then we have to find something acceptable to eat for a snack, like a Power Bar. So we nibble on a teeny-weeny bar and try to convince ourselves how satisfied we feel. Not. Next we rustle up some salt-free, nonbuttered popcorn. Foraging in our cupboards, we only come up with wheat-free, unsalted rice crackers made with seaweed. Then we sit around for the rest of the evening depressed as hell because we're so hungry. I tell you one thing—we may be healthy, but our diet is killing us!

---

4. Or arteries.

TEN

The Rules:

You've Got Male

A FEW YEARS AGO, two women cashed in big time with their homespun advice book that told you how to find the right man and then get him to marry you. The book was called *The Rules,* and everywhere you went, women of all ages were talking about it. I read it myself, and my feeling is that the advice is really nothing new, just an updated version of what our mothers have always told us.

However, it really made me aware of the fact that

women will follow advice from just about anybody out there who calls herself a "relationship expert." You've got to question the qualifications of such "experts" who appear regularly on TV trash talk shows advising, say, a nineteen-year-old unmarried girl about how to get the father of her three kids to marry her.

Now, I don't mean to brag, but I am about as qualified as anyone else to give my two cents' worth. After all, I have been married for twenty-five years,[1] which makes me somewhat of an expert just on the basis of longevity. But the difference between me and the relationship experts is that I am going to cut through all the B.S. and give it to you straight. There are a lot of slugs out there and women of any age need to know what's up. So here are Jan's Rules for the bagging and feeding of any conscious male in today's market. My ten "Rules According to Jan" will help you not only cut to the chase but also become a leading contender in it.

Rule 1. Never tell a boyfriend about your past sexual history.

One major problem with women who fall madly in love is they consider every guy their "soul mate." They feel compelled to "share" their past experiences about every lover in great detail. They also think that telling the pres-

---

1. To three different men.

ent boyfriend he is far superior to all their former lovers makes it perfectly okay. And it is—for a while. The new guy is in such a state of sexual ecstasy that initially, he feels flattered and it doesn't bother him. But watch out. After the newness wears off, all this stuff backfires more violently than Dom DeLuise in a refried-bean factory.

From now on, every single guy that crosses your path will be considered a threat. It will start off innocently enough, like with him saying, "Did I notice you smiling at that good-looking guy in the restaurant?" Then it progresses to "I don't like the way you hugged that guy at the party." And finally, "Listen, you slut, I remember what you said about shagging those other guys."

Uh-oh, Houston, you've got a problem. Now, no matter what you do, nothing will erase that scarlet A painted on your chest. You could be out doing volunteer work with Mother Teresa and you're going to get accused of sleeping with the lepers.

Therefore, my first rule in any relationship is: *Keep your mouth shut.*

You never had a past. You never dated. You never slept with a guy before. You think an orgasm is a germ. You can barely locate your own sex organs, much less anybody else's. You think your G-spot is a chord on your piano. Get my drift?

Rule 2. Pretend you love sports.

Women must realize that men are complex, multi-faceted, cerebral human beings. This is aptly demonstrated by their common pursuit of the same three lofty goals: beer, sports, and sex. Oh yeah, it really takes a genius to figure guys out. Put them in front of a football game with a beer in one hand and a woman in the other and they will remain in a contented stupor for the rest of their lives. You'll never have to worry about any guy straying when these three needs are being met. So Rule 2 is to learn as much about sports as you can and learn to fake liking it. This should not be difficult, since most women have already become experts at faking it in another area.[2]

Rule 3. Act helpless.

There is nothing a guy likes more than to act as a girl's protector. Guys love helpless women. It's in their big testosterone-filled nature to play the hero to every damsel in distress. So even if you work out in the gym seven days a week and have bigger biceps than he does, wear a long-sleeve dress to cover them up.

Remember, you are a female. Your brain has turned to mush from the sheer excitement of being with this

2. Du-uh-uh.

wonderful man. Men really hate independent women. This is evidenced by the fact that whenever they have to deal with a confident, self-assured woman, they call her a bitch. They think that any woman who can do for herself and doesn't need a man is a lesbian. So don't be afraid to cling and whine. It won't push them away. The only place they're going is on an ego trip.

Rule 4. Don't introduce him to your family right away.

Guys all think alike. If a man sees anyone in your family who has any kind of defect, he starts thinking that someday you are going to be just like that person. I had a good friend who was engaged to a beautiful girl for seven years. But he never married her because she had a really fat mother and he was always afraid that she would eventually balloon out like her someday.

The truth is that every family has its own crop of slightly tainted apples. You might have a klepto sister or an aunt with a giant butt, or your mom may have a police record. You know—little things. And rest assured, the guy is going to take one look at them and be *convinced* that in a few years you will become a fat-assed klepto with a police record. So keep those relatives under wraps[3] for as long as you can.

---

3. Or in a body bag.

Rule 5. Don't marry a student.

Medical, dental, law—it doesn't matter. Here's the drill. You will spend the best part of your life slaving to put him through school. You will look old before your time from working countless hours and going without the necessities of life,[4] sacrificing everything for his career. And when he finally graduates and can start being the breadwinner, you think your day has finally come.

Not in your dreams. Ninety percent of the time these ingrates turn around and tell you that they have "outgrown" you and are "too educated" for you, or you're "too old" and not "stimulating enough" for them anymore. Then they'll throw you over for a twenty-two-year-old bimbo named Bambi, whose greatest achievement other than her eighth-grade education is her forty-inch bust.

Rule 6. Don't look for guys in a bar.

It always amazes me that if a woman picks up a guy in a bar and later discovers he's an alcoholic, she's shocked. Well, du-uh-uh. What did you expect? Do most "normal" people sit there, socking back martinis with a boilermaker chaser at 3 P.M.? These guys are in there for one reason. They all have problems they're trying to forget.

So be warned. Bars are filled with guys who were

4. Facials, manicures, and face peels.

wounded in action. Do yourself a favor and stay as far away from the bar scene as you can. The last thing you need is a guy who is not only boozed up but also loaded down with more baggage than the carousel at United Airlines.

Rule 7. Don't get involved with a divorced man who has kids.

There are two words that describe a divorced guy with kids: guilt-ridden. Although he will declare that you will be number one in his life, the truth is that you will always come after his kids, his ex-wife, and all the ex–in-laws who are still fighting over the division of property. Contrary to what he tells you, the number one question on every divorced guy's mind is: Is this the woman I want my children to spend their weekends with?

Rule 8. Get breast implants.

There is one irrefutable law of nature: big boobs mean power. There isn't a guy on the planet who won't do anything, and I mean anything, to be with a girl who has big breasts. And they don't have to be real, either. They can be silicone, saline, or even sponge rubber. It doesn't matter as long as they are big. Oh sure, men try to deny it and say it's what's on the inside that counts. And they mean it too, as long as there's enough there to make a D cup.

Rule 9. Avoid men who are in therapy.

Trying to forge a relationship with a man who is in therapy is never a good idea. If a guy has more invested in his psychiatrist than his IRA, he's a bad choice. Granted, there are lots of legitimate reasons why a guy can be in therapy, but none of them bode well for you.

If he's trying to work out his insecurities, he'll want you to play the role of protector to him. Needy men are like black holes that suck all the life out of you. He will have to be reassured every second, like Stuart Smalley, that he's good enough, smart enough, and, gosh darn it, people like him. And what if he's an obsessive-compulsive? Think Jack Nicholson in *As Good As It Gets* and you've got the picture. You'll arrive late for everything because he'll have to wash his hands 200 times and go through the same doorway 150 times before you leave. Analyze this.

Rule 10. Keep the wedding plans low-key.

Nothing scares men more than a bunch of frenzied women planning a huge wedding. When you start using intimidating words like "peau de soie," "alençon lace," and "stephanotis," he's going to tune you out. Then, when he realizes that he's going to be the center of attention surrounded by a bridal party of twenty-four, an army of relatives, and a twenty-five-piece orchestra, he'll freak.

Guys just don't want a big fuss around them. They don't want to be thrown into the middle of all the problems a wedding creates, like bickering bridesmaids, in-laws with grudges, or friends who feel slighted. And when the guest list hits 250, even the best of men have been known to crumble and cancel the wedding.

My advice is to forget the white doves, strolling fiddlers, and six-tier cake. Take the money and use it as a down payment on a condo. Then go for a simple setting any guy will feel comfortable in—like one of those Vegas wedding chapels run by a minister in a tight white jumpsuit, aviator glasses, and an Elvis pompadour.

ELEVEN

Communication Competition:
Phone Envy

L AST WEEK I WENT TO LUNCH with a group of girlfriends, and from the looks of it, you would think
we were a Sprint convention. Ten women were
yakking furiously with each other across the table and
simultaneously answering their cell phones, which were

ringing off the hook every thirty seconds. And to make matters worse, their cell phones didn't ring like normal phones. Most of them were programmed to ring with those cutesy little tunes, like "La Cucaracha" or "I'm a Yankee Doodle Dandy."

There was just no way you could finish even one sentence with any gal before her phone rang and she excused herself to take the call. What's more, in between phones ringing, there were beepers going off, too. It was like being in a room filled with telemarketers. Pass the Valium.

What the heck can be so crucial that these women need to take calls every two minutes? They were getting calls from their kids, hairdressers, florists, relatives, husbands, other girlfriends, and just about anyone else with the same need for instant gratification. I began to wonder how on earth these women ever survived a single day before cell phones. They must have felt more isolated than Ginger on *Gilligan's Island*.

They also probably required therapy three times a week just to have somebody to talk with on a regular basis. Excuse me. Am I the only one out there who thinks this practice is not only excessive but also rude behavior? People think nothing of carrying on conversations during a movie or answering a call in the middle of a seminar.[1]

---

1. On the art of listening.

I especially hate it when I'm at a critical point in recounting something important that happened at my gynecologist's, and all of a sudden my girlfriend says, "Oh my gosh—excuse me—but I just remembered something really important. I've got to call Dagmar about scheduling my bikini wax for tomorrow. She'll be gone in ten minutes and I can't miss her."

It's either this scenario or else somebody's sister is calling long distance in a state of total panic because her au pair just quit. So there go fifteen more minutes, wasted on yet another issue of utter inconsequence. I don't know about you, but if it was me getting that call, I'd end that conversation on the spot with a few well-chosen words: "Get over it and watch your own kid."

But it doesn't stop here. More is better. I know women who actually carry two cell phones in their purses, one for regular calls and the other for business calls. Talk about unfinished conversations! Lunch isn't lunch anymore. It's like going to the O.K. Corral armed with a Colt .45 on each hip. Allow me to pose the obvious question. Is all this phone stuff really necessary?

Here is a recent luncheon conversation, typical of most of my lunches these days. A girlfriend needed my advice about some big problem that came up in her marriage. So I told her sure, I'd be glad to play shrink.

Well, I never had a chance to hear a coherent story
because the conversation went like this:

FRANNY: I'm at the end of my rope with Ken. Last
night he came storming in from work
and—(*Ring . . . ring . . . to the annoying tune
of "Old MacDonald Had a Farm"*)

FRANNY: Sorry. I better get this. Hello? Brittany?
What's the problem, baby? You didn't eat
your sandwich because . . . Why? . . . It
was the crunchy kind of peanut butter?
Mommy's sorry. Mommy will make the
noncrunchy kind tomorrow. Yes, honey
. . . Yes, sweetie . . . We'll talk about it at
home . . . Okay. . . . Gotta go . . . Gotta go
. . . Yep . . . Yep . . . Love you too . . . Bye.

FRANNY: (*Turning her attention to me*) Now, where
were we?

JAN: You were saying that Ken came home
and—

FRANNY: Okay, so Ken comes home mad at *me*
because his bitchy sister called him at

work and had the nerve to tell him
that—(*Ring . . . Ring . . . e–i–e–i–o*)

FRANNY: Oh, brother. I can't believe this. Sorry. Yes,
Sylvie . . . Yes, Sylvie . . . Well, where
exactly are these blisters? . . . Uh-huh . . .
Uh-huh . . . And what did the doc . . .
Uh-huh . . . Uh-huh . . . And he thinks it's
what? . . . Yeah . . . No . . . I don't know
. . . Is that a good thing or a bad thing?
. . . But . . . But . . . Sylvie, can I call you
later? I'm having lunch with a . . . Uh-
huh . . . Um . . . Okay. . . . Buh-bye.

FRANNY: (*Rolling her eyes*) You don't even want to
know what that was all about. So now
where was I?

JAN: (*Showing exasperation*) You were telling me
that the bitch . . . Ken's sister called him
and—

FRANNY: (*Interrupting*) Right. But first, here's the
scoop about why that three-hundred-
pound psycho-bitch is on my case. There's

been bad blood for years. And now, she's on this revenge thing from hell because I didn't invite her to my son's wedding last month. So yesterday, she calls Ken, and you won't believe this, she tells him that— (*Beep . . . Beep . . . Beep . . . Pager alert!*)

FRANNY: Oh, oh. I'm getting paged. Let me see . . . It's my real estate office. Must be about the escrow I'm closing on. Sorry again, but I have to call them immediately . . . Just take a sec . . .

JAN: (*Thinking*) Am I bleepin' invisible here?

AND SO IT GOES FOR OVER AN HOUR. This is what lunch has degenerated to in today's techno-driven society. I am left not only alone at the table but with dangling participles and a headache to boot. I am also left with unanswered questions with no resolution. What did the bitch say to Ken? Is Ken a weenie or a bully? Is the sister-in-law really a psycho-bitch from hell or is it just Franny? My God. It's no wonder I have to go home and load up on Xanax.[2] The only thing worse than cell

---

2. With a Thorazine chaser.

phones at lunch are cell phones in a moving vehicle. Every time I look out the car window, it seems like I see a frenzied woman gabbing on the phone while trying to read a map and making a left-hand turn in traffic—all at the same time. These women need to post one of those yellow signs in the rear window that says: DANGER ... DRIVER IS PHONE IMPAIRED.

Driving demands that you have all your wits about you. How can people dial phone numbers, hold a phone, and talk while attempting to steer a car? And what about those ditsy bimbos who are talking while applying eye shadow and nail polish, and taking the rollers out of their hair? Let's just pray they're not having phone sex, too, or we're really doomed.

TWELVE

Lengthy Labors:
Stand and Deliver

A NYTIME WOMEN GET TOGETHER for coffee, lunch, or any sort of gabfest, the conversation ultimately turns to stories about their labor and deliveries. Any woman who has ever experienced a six-centimeter or more dilation should automatically be awarded the Purple Heart for combat duty. Even though men serve on the battlefield, what women experience during labor and delivery is ten times worse.

Men are always bragging about how tough they

are, but their war stories pale in comparison to ours. However, it gives them a testosterone rush to sit around, drink beer, and talk blood and brawn on the battlefield. And when relating their war stories, men are the total masters of one-upsmanship. I know this for a fact, because when I was a kid and went to the American Legion with my dad, I used to listen to conversations like this:

> GOMER 1: Back in forty-two during "The Big One," I got my right arm and left leg shot up in twenty-three places. Shattered the bones so bad, I was in a body cast for three years. To this day, it still hurts like a son-of-a-bitch to lift a bottle of beer.

> GOMER 2: Oh, yeah? Well, when I was in Germany, I took six bullets in the face and a grenade in the left flank. Lost thirty-six feet of intestine. Since then, every time I burp, it comes out through my ears.

I know that I'm speaking for all women when I say, "Big deal." If you really want to hear about blood, guts, and gore, nothing compares with the labor and delivery stories women have been privy to over the years from our mothers, grandmothers, and aunts. And after listening to their litany on a weekly basis while growing up, it's a miracle any one of us actually got pregnant.[1]

One of the all-time classic childbirth stories came from my Grandma Prahovic, who gave birth to all seven children at home. Grandma was an immigrant from Croatia back in the days before CNN or Dan Rather discovered it. Anyway, she gave birth to her sixth kid on the staircase when she was coming down to cook kielbasa and sauerkraut in the kitchen. This may not have been your most sterile environment for a delivery, but at least there was a pot of water boiling on the stove. Although nobody has ever been able to explain what the boiling water is actually used for, you know you've got to have it. Why, fiddle-dee-dee, even Scarlett O'Hara had it when "birthing" her baby.[2]

So when Grandma popped her sixth out right there on the stairs, at least she had some boiling water on hand. I always wanted to ask if she cut the cord with the same knife she used on the kielbasa, but in those days etiquette and the fear of getting a good sock in the teeth prohibited young ladies from asking such personal questions.

Can you imagine delivering a baby all by yourself in

---

1. We obviously had the pants scared off us.

2. She didn't know nuthin' 'bout birthin' no babies.

an upright position? I don't know about you, but I can't even unwrap a Fruit Roll-Up without assistance. My Grandma was a trouper, that's for sure. The small town where she lived had only one family doctor who made house calls.[3] And he always arrived a few hours after the blessed event, just in time for dinner. It was rumored that Grandma did in fact serve him kielbasa and sauerkraut after resting up for an hour. You go, Grandma.

So what did I learn from this family saga? Three things:

1. I was descended from stock tougher than Brahman bulls.
2. The aroma of simmering kielbasa makes me throw up.
3. I should live in a one-story home.

Not to be outdone by the kielbasa and sauerkraut saga, my mom had a better one up her sleeve. I heard this story more times than I cared to and spent a lifetime trying to repress it. My mom delivered my brother during the war years, when anesthesia was called 80 proof. She allegedly lay there in the bed, writhing and screaming in labor, for thirty-six hours before finally giving birth. My brother was delivered by low forceps, which forced his

3. A practice that has become extinct.

head to take on the same shape as Beldar's from *The Coneheads.*

This compelled my grandmother to spend the better part of the next six months massaging his pointy little head in hopes of achieving a natural humanoid sphere. Thankfully, nature took its course and he turned out just fine. However, as a kid, I just reveled in this information. It gave me fabulous ammunition for a retaliatory strike when my brother mercilessly teased me. You can just imagine how many times the phrase "you pointy-headed moron" came up over fifteen years.

In those days, the kind of drugs they gave you during delivery were the kind that knocked you out until your kid was in the first grade. Before that, women had no other recourse but to bite the bullet and suffer through long labors. And even though we never heard the end of how much pain our moms went through, when it was our turn to give birth, they all developed a convenient case of amnesia. Then they spouted the same well-rehearsed phrase about labor: "Don't worry—it's the kind of pain you forget." Oh yeah? If that's so, why can every woman who ever gave birth recall in excruciating detail every cramp, contraction, and gut-wrenching push she had over thirty years ago? And why is it that the women in *National Geographic* dig holes in the ground, squat, deliver a baby, and go back to work fifteen minutes later? All the stories I've ever heard about giving birth in our advanced country are filled with references of pain and extreme violence: like women screaming, fainting, and smacking their husbands around the delivery room.

I was twenty-eight years old when I delivered my first child. My labor began six weeks earlier than expected, too. I was sitting out on my back porch occupying all three seats on the couch when my water broke. At first I thought I must have been losing bladder control, because I had lost control over pretty much everything else in my body for the last 7½ months.

I had no idea what it was like when your water broke. It's not just a little trickle thing going on, either. Mine was more like a geyser that actually produced a moat around the foundation of my house. Thankfully, it was the seventies and I was wearing my fashionable vinyl go-go boots. So after I waded through the moat and did a quick wipe-off, I headed for the hospital. No boiling water, no kielbasa, no sauerkraut for me.

Once I got to the hospital, I was placed on a gurney and lay there, leaking like a defective Gladbag. My O.B. was still at home watching a Redskins game. Testosterone gives way for no one. When he finally arrived and examined me, he found that my amniotic sac wasn't completely ruptured. He told me he would finish breaking it with a surgical instrument. You can imagine my shock when he pulled out a giant stainless-steel hook for the job. Thinking back, I realize it was an exact duplicate that the serial killer carried in *I Know What You Did Last Summer.* Suddenly, I felt as vulnerable as Jennifer Love Hewitt in a thong. I scrunched my eyes shut and prayed he didn't make any false moves.

One thing I was totally adamant about was that there be no cameras of any kind in the delivery room. Why would any woman want to have her picture taken when she is all messed up and sweating like a pig with her legs stretched apart in different time zones? Forget about it. When my husband first approached me about filming the birth I told him, "You film my delivery and I'll film your vasectomy."

Since when did childbirth become such a voyeuristic event? Try to find one flattering angle during this ordeal. These pictures are not exactly suitable material for your family album, either. Then after I was wheeled into the delivery room, they asked if I wanted to watch the birth from one of the large mirrors on the wall. They had to be kidding. I asked for a blindfold.

To speed up my labor, they gave me Pitocin. This is a drug that makes the uterus contract hard and fast. When the contractions became really painful, I began screeching in octaves even Mariah Carey has never hit.

I begged for medication—which was not a politically correct move when you're supposed to be toughing it out with Lamaze. The nurses kept telling me to do my "pant-blow" technique. At this point, I was about as willing to pant-blow as I was to get up and perform the second act of Riverdance.[4]

After I reached the magic ten-centimeter milestone, I began to experience the sensation of "pushing." This is when it feels like a St. Bernard is trying to come through a cat door. The nurses kept telling me not to push. Why, I have no idea. But I suspect it must have had something to do with the fourth-quarter tie score at RFK Stadium. Let me tell you something. Trying not to push was about as easy as trying to hold back Joe Montana as he thunders down the field to score a touchdown. The "push" is a force of nature and is impossible to hold off—kind of like a teenage boy in the backseat of a car.

By now, I was in such pain that I was beginning to see a bright light and all my dead relatives waving at me. As soon as my anesthesiologist came through the door, I told him to get the gas mask on me fast or he was a dead man. When I finally felt it cover my mouth and nose, I sucked all the gas out of the canister in one gulp.

---

4. In the nude.

The guy in *Blue Velvet* had nothing on me. And just before I drifted off to la-la land, I remember thinking: *"Note to self: get tubes tied."*

THIRTEEN

The Gynecologist:
A Deeper Look

L ADIES, I THINK THERE'S NO QUESTION that we are one
tough species. However, there is one event that can
reduce us to a collective quivering mass of Jell-O and
send us hyperventilating into our Kate Spade tote bags.
You got it—our appointments with the gynecologist.
You would think we'd get used to it after the first few
thousand times or so. Why not? I guess we really can't
put our finger on it, and if the truth were known, we
don't want our doctors to, either.

We are all aware that the second worst kept secret since Monica Lewinsky is that no gynecologist could ever be accused of being punctual. Many a woman has actually gone through menopause in the waiting room. And we feel even older when we see all those young, pregnant women. It's also really easy to spot the gals who are trying to get pregnant. They're the ones with the thermometers hanging out of their mouths and the ovulation charts pinned to their chests.

The receptionist hands you "a few forms" to fill out with detailed questions about your medical insurance and medical history. Be prepared to wade through a stack of paperwork the likes of which hasn't been seen since the Trump divorce settlement. You'll also have to answer all kinds of really personal questions when filling out your medical history. Here's a sample:

1. Did you ever fail a Pap test? (Did you study for it?)
2. Do you always wear your diaphragm? (Are you wearing it now?)
3. Have you had sex with multiple partners? (At the same time?)
4. Does your partner wear condoms? (At the office?)
5. Is intercourse with a condom sometimes painful? (Do you always remember to remove the wrapping?)

6. Are your breasts frequently sore or painful? (Is your bra too small?)

7. Is douching often painful? (Do you use a jet spray?)

8. Have you experienced persistent itching? (Did you try a dandruff shampoo?)

9. Would you mind permitting a few ob-gyn interns to be present in the room to watch your exam? (On *Springer*?)

10. Do you suspect you might have a yeast infection? (Are you sprouting muffins?)

When you finally hear the words "The doctor will see you now," it's show time. Your body reacts with a fifty-point spike in your blood pressure plus an over-stimulation of your sweat glands. In fact, you'll be sweating so profusely, you'll have to wring out your dress shields in the bathroom. Once you're in there, the nurse will ask you to perform two impossible feats that even the great Houdini never mastered:

1. To fill a urine specimen bottle with a .0001 millimeter neck and avoid any spillage.[1]

2. To hide your naked butt under a paper examination gown barely large enough to cover a sardine.

---

1. It's helpful to wear rubber boots.

After you're led into the examination area, the nurse will instruct you to lie down on a steel table in a room whose temperature has never risen above thirty degrees Fahrenheit. By now, you're thinking, "Does Blue Cross cover frostbite?"[2] Next, she hikes your feet up into the stirrups[3] and then places a two-by-two-inch handkerchief-sized sheet over you. At this point, you are about as covered up as Susan Sarandon's breasts at the Academy Awards. You lie there, shivering like a hairless Chihuahua, for another forty-five minutes, until the doctor enters the room. He takes one look at your blue, frozen body and says to the nurse, "Are you sure this patient hasn't expired?"

Just before he begins your checkup, he'll ask for a recent photo of you, since this is the first and last time he'll ever be looking at your face. By now you're so nervous, you're wishing you had been tranquilized with a dart gun for this exam.

Most gynecologists have two really bad habits:

1. They insist on using a speculum that has just come out of the autoclave.

2. They use so much K-Y Jelly, you keep sliding off the examination table.

---

2. Not even in Alaska.

3. Hermes will cost you fifty bucks more.

They also tell you that the exam will not be painful. Oh, sure. I usually end up screaming my head off—and this is while he's still putting on the examination gloves. The speculum is bad enough, but the part I hate the most is when he starts probing around your ovaries. At this point, he innocently inquires, "Any pain or tenderness?" I'd like to reply, "Are you wearing your stethoscope too tight?" But I am incapable of answering because I have just ground my teeth into dust.

I always come to the office with a million questions I need answered but end up asking none of them. This is because I find it quite disconcerting to carry on a conversation with a man who is talking directly into my cervix. Besides, I am going through menopause and am lucky to remember my own name these days.

Just as you're ready to bolt out the door . . . not so fast. The nurse stops you dead in your tracks and asks if you've had your annual mammogram. No? Well, this is your lucky day. The doctor has just purchased a state-of-the art mammogram machine, the Chernobyl X5000. And it's in the next room in dire need of another patient to help pay it off. This time you are asked to remove everything above the waist. Then the nurse leads you, like a lamb to slaughter, toward this formidable-looking machine.

The X-ray tech explains that you will need to lay your breast on a cold, steel plate for the procedure.

What's up with all this cold stuff? Are these people afraid we'll decompose at room temperature? I guess the technicians are well trained, but personally I don't trust anybody wearing the same kind of badge that I see them wearing at McDonald's. And another thing. The term "mammogram" creeps me out. It sounds as though they're going to put stamps on your breasts and mail them somewhere.

To get the correct views for the imaging, the tech will have you twist your body into some very weird positions. In fact, I've seen some of the same contortions performed at Cirque du Soleil. And if you are well endowed, the tech will have to position your breast on the table for you—a task she performs with about the same enthusiasm as picking up roadkill. But worse yet, if you're a tiny AA cup, she might whisk out a magnifying glass to try to spot them. Once your breast is positioned properly, she pulls down a Lucite plate, which flattens your poor boob like a mangler in a dry cleaner's. At this point, you're probably thinking you'll have to roll them up to get them back into your bra.

All during this exam, the tech constantly reassures you this is a totally safe procedure. So tell me, why is the radiologist dressed in a lead apron and operating the machine behind a six-foot concrete wall? But the worst part is waiting to hear the results. You feel like "Frankie the Face" waiting on death row.

Good news! The radiologist says all is fine in mammyland. She attempts to explain your radiograph in layman's terms you can understand. She tells you to think of your X-rays as "breast maps." Then she says that yours are flatter than an interstate, have no visible potholes, and would be of no interest to the average road crew.

NOBODY CAN SAY that these exams aren't traumatic for a woman. And it really annoys me that men aren't subjected to the same kind of medical torture. They take a cavalier attitude about our being nervous before our gynecological exams. What hypocrites. Just watch the way they behave when their doctors suggest a prostate exam. Do you really think they're actually going to let a doctor do one on them? Most guys won't even let someone wave a finger in their face. They handle it exactly the way they do anything else unpleasant—by avoidance. The only time guys seek medical attention is when they have an acute problem—like decapitation.

FOURTEEN

Getting Your Way, Southern Style:

Kiss My Grits

M
Y MOMENT OF REVELATION happened on a hot,
humid day in Memphis, Tennessee. I was out in
the backyard with my two active boys, ages two
and four, running wildly all over the place. In an instant,

it became crystal clear to me that I was going about my life in all the wrong ways.

I was in my early thirties, raising two overactive boys and working a full-time job. I was also in the middle of the horrific task of sanding and painting the lawn furniture. Dressed in an old pair of raggedy jeans and a grimy T-shirt, I slaved away while sweat trickled down the back of my neck. I was wearing no makeup and my nails were ruined from the harsh chemicals and sandpaper. As I was yelling at my kids, who were being particularly monstrous that day, I happened to glance over the fence at my next-door neighbor, Scarlett O'Hara.

Of course her real name wasn't Scarlett, but she embodied everything "Scarlett" to me. So for the purpose of accommodating my mean streak, allow me to call her by that name. So here's Scarlett sitting on her beautiful azalea-intensive patio, drinking frosty lemonade out of a crystal glass and thumbing through *Southern Living*. She was wearing an organza pinafore, hair perfectly done in an upsweep with well-placed tendrils wisping down her neck, and was turning the pages with her perfectly manicured nails. Her two daughters were dressed in adorable matching outfits and were cutting out paper dolls with their nanny.

I looked at this scene and thought to myself, "As God is my witness, I'm watching Scarlett O'Hara living out her charmed life at Tara over there. And here I am, Rosie the Riveter, with dishpan hands and a bad attitude." Where the hell did I go wrong?

Let's review:

- I'm basically dressed in rags; she's lounging in Dior.
- My nails look like someone took a hacksaw to them; she gets a manicure and pedicure once a week.
- Her kids are playing like little ladies; mine are giving each other bloody noses and bruised butts.
- I am the babysitter, cook, handyman, and housecleaner; she hires separate people to do these jobs for her.
- She gets to live the life of Tara; mine is more like *Gone with the Wind* on mescaline.

As if this wasn't bad enough, here's the kicker: When my husband came home, I certainly received no accolades for doing all these jobs by myself, with no help. He expects it. He even complained that the dinner I cooked wasn't good. But when Scarlett's husband comes home, he'll bring her flowers. He will praise her for being a wonderful wife and mother and tell her how much gratitude he feels for her because she makes such a beautiful home for him.

DO I SOUND BITTER? You bet your bippy I do. I had to sit down and really think hard about this question. How do these women manage to have a life of ease but make it look like they're killing themselves for their husbands? Here's what I came up with. In a word—HELPLESS. Southern women are the absolute mistresses of acting helpless and needy, which makes their men feel like knights in shining armor whose mission it is to rescue them from all things perilous. Men love to play the hero. It feeds their egos. Smart women are aware of this and use it to their own advantage. Southern women were born with genes that have programmed them to do this perfectly.

Even before the Civil War, Northern women had it all wrong. We have an attitude that we can do it all. We pooh-pooh men for doing niceties for women and discourage their macho behavior. Wrong. And we're paying the price for it. Because we feel that we should have it all, we also think we have to do it all by ourselves to get it. We could all learn a lot from our Southern sisters. With the proper attitude, a gal can not only give a guy a ton of crap, but get away with it and come out smelling like a rose. Trust me. These women have their black belts in manipulation.

The following scenarios will show you the two modi operandi.

Case Study 1: The Child-Care Scenario

The kids are driving us bonkers. We feel like we never have a peaceful moment to ourselves. They even follow us into the bathroom, whining. They won't go to bed without a major fit. We're exhausted and feel like we're living out a prison sentence.

JAN: (*Complaining bitterly to her husband*) I'm really sick and tired of having to manage the boys by myself all day. Most of the time they act like monsters, continually fighting and screaming. They never mind me, no matter how loud I yell. I am totally exhausted. You don't understand how tough it is for me. I need a live-in to give me a break.

SCARLETT: (*Purring to her husband with a honey-coated voice*) Rhett, sweetie, lately ah've been thinkin' that ah want to have more time to be romantic with y'all. I have such a hankerin' for more alone time with you, sugah. Dahlin', we need more time to make love. Ah love the children but theah takin' up just a teeny-weeny bit too much time that ah could be spendin'

with you. Wouldn't it be just too wonderful if we had an au pair or a nanny?

P.S. Guess which one gets her way.[1]

The real story: Scarlett gets her au pair and spends all
her newly found free time either shopping at Neiman's
or going to bridge luncheons with the girls. She throws
Rhett a bone by giving him ten extra minutes a night
during which she plays to his ego by making promises of
upcoming sexual favors—which, of course, never mate-
rialize because she always develops a migraine.[2] But she
doesn't worry about it because—you got it—tomorrow
is another day![3]

Case Study 2: The Dereliction-of-Duty Scenario

Jan and Scarlett go out for lunch with a bunch of
gals to celebrate a girlfriend's birthday. As usual, the gals
really overdo it. They have too much wine, talk way too
long, and nobody wants to go home. They are having
just too damn much fun. When they get home too late
to prepare a decent dinner for their families, they both

---

1. Du-uh-uh.

2. She also has dysmenorrhea twenty-nine days a month.

3. And another excuse.

order pizzas. Jan catches holy hell. Scarlett gets a diamond bracelet. This is why.

JAN: (*Timidly in a defensive tone*) Gosh, I'm really sorry but we're going to have to order pizza for dinner. I was out for lunch with the girls and we were having such a good time that the whole afternoon just kind of slipped by. I know pizza isn't your favorite, but after all, I hardly ever get out. So I don't think that this is too much to ask from you.

SCARLETT: (*In a tone dripping with sucrose*) Rhett, dahlin', guess what? Ah'm plannin' a sizzlin' evenin' just for us. Ah ordered pizza and Coca-Cola and we'll pretend like we're datin' again. Remembah when we ate pizza and made out all night? Well, sugah, tonight we're gonna do it all over again.

The real story: Rhett wolfed down the pizza while the nanny put the kids to bed. Scarlett smooches with him for three minutes until she suddenly develops a bad toothache. She takes to her canopied bed, crying, begging

Rhett to sit by her side and administer Anbesol through an I.V. drip. He obliges with pleasure.

THE SECOND THING I NOTICED about Southern women is that none of them actually do their own housework. They all develop some strange hypochondriacal condition that prohibits them from doing any form of manual labor. Scarlett had an arsenal of such conditions. Dusting gave her migraines. Yard work aggravated her hay fever. Washing dishes exacerbated contact dermatitis. Mopping floors? Out of the question. Her slipped disk made any physical exertion, except for shopping, impossible. Furniture polish irritated her eyes. Changing diapers triggered her gag reflex. All cleaning products brought on heart palpitations. You name it, she had a condition to cover it.

But she would tell Rhett how much she wished she could do all the household chores so she could show him what a wonderful wife and mother she was. But her physical disabilities just wouldn't permit it. She so hated those horrid limitations that made her "weak as a kitten." Oh, yeah. A kitten with a whip. This woman managed to have a platoon of people who did everything possible for her—and her husband loved her all the more for it. Many people would call this behavior deceitful and selfish. I call it genius.

The third thing that Southern women are into heavily is denial. If they get bad news, they just go on with what they were saying as if they never heard it. Whether it's their kids, husbands, in-laws, or whoever is bugging them—it falls on deaf ears, baby. Just look at the way the same topic is handled by Northern versus Southern ladies:

RHETT: Jan, I'm really sorry but I have bad news for you. The wedding is off. I have realized that I cannot make a permanent commitment and walk down that aisle next week. I know you have your gown and sent out the invitations. Your parents have paid for the flowers, caterer, and reception hall. But it's better that I tell you now. I would end up being a terrible husband who probably would cheat on you. You deserve a lot better than that.

JAN: (*Hysterically crying*) Oh my God!!! What are you saying? I can't believe it. You love me. I love you. My parents have spent thousands on this wedding. Everything is ordered. I'll be humiliated. What is the problem? Whatever it is, I can change.

Am I too needy? I'll give you space. Too demanding? I'll back off. We'll go to counseling. You'll see. We'll work out whatever our problems are. Please tell me you don't mean this. Please . . . Sob, sob, grovel, grovel . . .

SCARLETT: (*Sits and listens to same spiel calmly and quietly. No interruptions. After a few minutes of silence, she demurely adds a sprig of mint to her iced tea. Lovingly batting her baby blues at him and softly cooing*) Rhett, dahlin' . . . do you want me to pick up the studs for your tuxedo tomorrow?

P.S. Guess which one is the bridesmaid and which one is the bride?

FIFTEEN

Sex After Marriage:

Romancing the Stone

S O HERE WE ARE, MIDDLE-AGED and facing the problem of how to remedy the doldrums in our flagging sex lives. And believe me, the flag is at half-mast. However, we baby boomers like to think that we haven't lost our sex drives, we've just misplaced them. So take heart. Help is just a credit card number away. Everywhere we turn these days, there are self-proclaimed sex gurus and relationship experts telling us what we should be doing to spice up our sex lives. I've listened to many, but let me tell you something—their advice is pretty far out. If we began practicing what they recommend, we'd die of exhaustion, overexposure, or severe abrasions—or all three.

Our generation came into its collective sexuality during the sixties and seventies. Our hormones were more out of control than Janis Joplin at Woodstock. Free love was the hip philosophy back then. It was a sexual feeding frenzy. And here's the unbelievable part—we did it in *broad daylight*. We didn't care where we were—on the beach, in the ocean, the woods. There was a lot more than the sound of one tree falling in the forest. Back in the seventies, people went down faster than Kamikazis.

And name me a time when we didn't have the urge. But nowadays—ugh!—don't get me started. By middle age, we have so much to hide—starting with our crow's feet.[1] So the love light has dimmed considerably over the years. Now we find ourselves making love in a room that's so dark it looks like the Bat Cave.

At our age, it's almost impossible to find a flattering position for our aging bodies. There's no way we're going to lie flat on our backs and have that thigh-spread thing going on. We also have to avoid being on top because it makes our faces look like someone let the air

---

1. Those are just the ones on our thighs, for openers.

out of them. We've also got cellulite bumps popping out more frequently than teenage zits. What a mess. No wonder phone sex has become so popular in the last few years.

Lengthy foreplay has also become just a memory. It just takes too much effort. Even after ten minutes of that stuff, I'm so exhausted, I look like a dehydrated runner who has just crossed the tape at the Boston Marathon. So what else can we do to give it some zip? It's like hamburger—there's a limit to how many different ways you can serve it.

However, the experts are making a great living out of trying. And all of them preach the same message: 101 ways to put the passion back in your sex life. I've always been curious as to why it's always 101 ways. What is it about that number? I'm not sure I can learn to do anything 101 ways, much less have sex. I, for one, don't put much credence in any of these gurus or their message du jour. Instead, I believe we have to analyze how we learned about sex and what we expected from it. Then we should compare it to what we actually got. And I think we'll find that it's a chasm wider than when Moses parted the Red Sea.

Women boomers had no real source of sexual education back in the Puritan days. About the only resource we had was Harlequin Romance novels. We bought those books by the caseful, eager to learn how virgins were conquered through the ages. And it was steamy stuff for those days! They always wrote about how a virgin with various pulsating parts waited for her white knight to "take her" as she lay breathlessly[2] on her lace bed strewn with rose petals.

And the heroine-virgin always had a hyphenated name, like Lady Sherwin-Williams. Then there was an entire chapter devoted to the virgin "soaring" to the heights of Olympus when the hero conquered her, body and soul. One thing you can say about the fifties was that virgins didn't give it up easily. It took at least six chapters.

The prevailing philosophy has always been that women need a *reason* to have sex. Guys just need a *place.* The guys of the boomer generation all received their sexual education from three sources. The first was the streets, from a buddy who appointed himself the official sex aficionado. At sixteen years of age, he boasted that he had already had hundreds of sexual experiences. What he failed to mention was they all happened while he was alone. The second source was the ever-popular porno films, called "smokers" back then. Guys have always thought that porno films were the same thing as watching a beautiful romance movie with the boring

2. Those corsets were brutal.

parts taken out. These films also had the added advantage of having very little dialogue to pay attention to. God forbid that anybody confuses them during their educational process.

The third educational tool was *Playboy* magazine, the classic text for guys. Long live Hugh Hefner. Even though he's seventy-three years old now, every guy still wants to trade places with him. Recently divorced, Hef's bragging about dating some hot twins from Illinois. Really. It's probably Dear Abby and Ann Landers. I think the magazine has always been and still is the all-time most significant source of misinformation about women and their sexual habits. From the pictorials alone, guys were left with the impression that women spend most of the day lounging on the couch with their legs stuck up in the air, wearing nothing but a garter belt and fishnet stockings. Not only that, but they also believe that it's a common occurrence for us to wash dishes in nothing but an apron and five-inch stiletto heels.

So when the boomer guys and gals finally got together, was it any wonder that our first sexual experiences were disasters? We gals were expecting ecstasy on our lace and lavender sheets, while the guys expected to get laid on Naugahyde car seats. What a mess. And ever since then, women have been forced to deal with their disappointments while trying to reconcile their concepts of romance and sex. We longed for a hopelessly romantic man just like the ones pictured on the covers of our romance novels.[3] But we usually had to settle for the kind on the cover of *Popular Mechanics.*

But I guess by middle age, many of us feel that any sex is better than no sex at all. So whom else should we turn to for help? If you seek medical advice, many doctors will prescribe the male hormone testosterone to increase a woman's sex urge. But I'm skeptical. I've heard that your sex life gets better but you have to shave every time you make love. Some holistic practitioners recommend herbs like chasteberry or soy products and yam creams. I guess there's no harm in these because if it doesn't work you can always concoct a nutritious salad.

I don't know if I'm ready or willing to do all the things the sex gurus recommend to perk up your passion. First of all, I refuse to greet my husband at the door every day wrapped in plastic like the protective covering of my grandmother's couch. I also don't want to go through the trouble of having to write little love notes and hide them in his underwear drawer. He'll never find them, anyway, because after showering he puts the same pair back on.

---

3. Fabio—without the seagull stuck on his face.

I refuse to follow those silly love manuals that instruct you to make love in a different room every night. At my age, I'm having trouble just finding the bathroom at 1 A.M. I also hate it when they tell women we have to act like the aggressors during sex because it turns men on. So what *doesn't* turn men on? Every woman knows that men make all major decisions with their penises. I'm not going to dress up in some slutty Victoria's Secret corset with whalebones that forces my boobs up so far they double as ear flaps. I'm sure I'd pass out from oxygen deprivation and miss the whole event. Though, I'm not sure if this is a good thing or a bad thing.

Presently, many of my divorced girlfriends are having fabulous sex for the first time in their lives. You should listen to them talk about it—it's nauseating.[4] But I also have to tell you that they are dating and having sex with much younger guys. I can imagine the thrills must be fabulous, but I wouldn't want to have sex with a guy I have to drop off at school really early the next morning. I also wouldn't be caught dead in a prom gown—no matter how great the sex was.

Maybe the answer is pharmaceutical. After all, this is the age of chemical romance. There's a pill to stimulate just about every primitive urge we possess. Drugs

---

4. After the first eight hours.

like rohypnol, ecstasy, and Viagra are being sold legally and illegally everywhere you turn. They'll give you the urge anytime you want. And I'll say one thing. It's a lot easier than having to dress up in a French maid costume and role-play all evening just to get it on. It's also a lot easier than trying to execute eighty-five different positions from the Kama Sutra. Not to mention the chiropractor's bills. All I know is that I'm really confused. Thinking about all this stuff gives me a headache. Oh yeah—I've already used that one about a million times . . . anyone for a spanking?

SIXTEEN

Dieting:
Lean and Really Mean

W HEN GALS SIT AROUND stuffing their faces at lunch, the number one topic of conversation is always dieting. I don't think there's another subject that even comes close in terms of hours spent yakking about how much we need to lose weight. But unfortunately, that's all we do—talk. I can't tell you how many times I've heard the merits of the Atkins diet versus the Zone diet. Not to mention the juice, water, cabbage soup, algae, or just about any other cockamamie regimen some housewife from Bayonne has managed to get published after a six-martini lunch with a fledgling editor. So we read and talk, talk and read. But doing the actual dieting is another story. It takes most of us quite a while to get around to that part—like, at least until the dawning of another millennium.

Over the course of a year, a woman's weight is up and down more times than Pamela Anderson Lee's marriage is on and off. We all have a closet filled with "fat clothes." We all complain about how the cleaner has shrunk every last pair of our jeans. We have had our clothes taken in and let out so many times, they have tread marks. There's no weight control center, diet book, or fad diet we haven't investigated. But after making some initial attempt, we always get into the yo-yo situation where we lose a few pounds, then end up gaining it all back—and then some.

My problem with diet books is that most of them are written by women with the body fat of a whippet, or by gorgeous stars like Suzanne Somers, Victoria Principal, and Marilu Henner. What are they doing writing about diets? Now I ask you, who can relate to these women? The only thing that would be more ludicrous is when Calista Flockhart comes out with her first diet book.[1]

---

1. *Ally McBeal Needs an Ally McMeal.*

That's it. Then I'm gonna kill myself. Why are these women writing about dieting? They've never even experienced gaining two extra pounds, much less dealt with a cellulite bump. And if they did develop one, they'd run like hell to their plastic surgeons and have it immediately removed. What we need is a diet book from somebody who has been there—like Roseanne. I wouldn't even mind if one of her alternate personalities wrote it. To tell the truth, she's looking pretty good these days—all twenty-three of her.

USUALLY THE MOTIVATION you need to lose weight is a monumental event—like your twenty-fifth high school reunion. This is when the weight-loss issue is accorded its proper status—life or death. At your reunion, it's imperative that you make an entrance looking as thin and youthful as possible. After all, you'll be socializing with a lot of old people who claim they were your classmates.

Another huge motivator to shed those extra pounds is summer. The thought of trying on bathing suits, shorts, or sleeveless blouses after a long winter of hot chocolate and s'mores is truly a frightening one. Believe me, when you're trying on a bathing suit in that little dressing room with the fun-house mirrors and fluorescent lighting, it's the pits. No. It's worse than the pits—it's an abyss.

When you first catch a glimpse of yourself in the mirror, you'll feel like asking the salesgirl to bring in a loaded firearm along with your XXL garment. You're staring at a body that has been hibernating all winter, storing fat. It's morphed beyond cave-bear into whale-sized proportions. In fact, you'll probably think that you make Moby Dick look like a sardine. It's enough to make you go home and subsist on mung beans for the next six months.

Last year I chose to get into shape. Unfortunately, the shape I chose was an oval. But it didn't take me long to grow tired of having the waistline of a Teletubby. So I tried counting calories on my own. But that didn't work. My entire existence became one giant sacrifice, and even then, I only managed to lose a couple of measly pounds. It was depressing as hell. I considered one of those liquid diets but abandoned that idea pretty fast. Who wants to drink meals through a straw? I'm going to be doing that when I'm seventy-five, anyway.

Then I ran into a girlfriend who had just lost twenty pounds and looked great. She did it by going to a popular diet center, and she looked so good, it inspired me to get off my buns of flab and go for it, too. But I had no idea what I was in for. These places are run like a military academy. They assigned me a German counselor, Dr. Ruthless, who made Dr. Mengele look like Dr. Seuss. The woman was so brutal she thought of the

Spanish Inquisition as tough love. It was hard to relate to her on any level. Besides, she didn't speak very good English. And unfortunately, all the German I know I learned from *Hogan's Heroes.*

The first thing she did was take a personal history in which I was asked to write about my eating habits. It snapped me into the reality that I was living in lipid land. We're talking about consuming french fries that contain more oil than potato and more salt than the Dead Sea. Or how about those Taco Bell burrito grandes I'd been putting away all year? Not to mention corn chips that had been submerged in a hot tub filled with lard—now there's a cardiovascular treat. It's a wonder I hadn't heard my arteries hardening as I ate.

Dr. Ruthless began our first session by showing me a motivational film and giving me some bottled water— one drop at a time. I must admit her technique didn't do much to solidify our bonding. She also gave me her pat speech about sticking to the diet with no deviations. I was only allowed the foods on her list and had to sign an affidavit saying I'd never eat between meals again. She warned me that she'd be watching. She'd know every move I made. And just to make sure, she strapped one of those electric devices around my ankle to monitor where I went. One false move toward Baskin-Robbins and I was toast. Zapped to the asphalt in seconds.

I quickly realized that this place was a glorified starvation camp. I was put on a 200-calorie-a-day regimen and had to purchase precooked and -measured meals, packaged in pathetic little foil pouches. I took them everywhere, from dinner parties to luncheons. I began to feel like a homeless woman, crashing all of my own social events.

The worst part about these regimented diets is that they make you feel so deprived. I found myself salivating as I watched my girlfriends eating greasy Reuben sandwiches and pouring mountains of dressing on everything. There I would sit, staring at my .001-ounce piece of watercress. At this rate, I figured that after a month I'd have wasted away to nothing. They'd probably have to put my picture on a milk carton.

But I sat there, trying to make the best of my one green leaf and .009 ounce of skinless, boneless, meatless chicken breast. While all the women were feasting, I did my own version by chewing my one little piece of lettuce over and over, trying to make it last through a normal person's lunchtime. I felt like crying. Then it got worse. While all my friends ordered tiramisu for dessert, I actually contemplated a hemlock smoothie.[2]

After feeling like I'd spent two weeks in a

2. Nonfat, of course.

Vietnamese prison camp, I reported back to Dr. Ruthless. I got on the scale, stark naked, because we all know that our underpants add at least four pounds. And—oh, no—I had lost only 1.2 pounds. I dissolved into tears. But Dr. Ruthless slapped me and told me to get a grip.[3] What a nightmare. After another pep talk and a mild electrical shock, I felt the old resolve returning[4] and decided to hang in for another week. Just like Charlton Heston, I was sticking to my guns.

In the end, I was successful . . . sort of. I actually lost twelve pounds in six of the most stinking, lousiest, longest months of my life. But the problem was, when I no longer had Dr. Ruthless scaring me skinny, I put the weight back on in a matter of weeks. But the thought of returning to that little camp of horrors was just too much. I prayed for deliverance. At 3 A.M., when I was totally depressed and eating a low-fat fudge brownie, my prayers were answered. I happened to catch an infomercial for an amazing new pill that claims to "melt away" all the fat in your body. They guarantee you will lose up to five pounds a week with no side effects except some minor intestinal cramping and possible anal leakage.[5] The advertisers are

---

3. She had been trained by General Patton.

4. Along with my consciousness.

5. And you lose all of your friends.

well aware that anybody who is up at 3 A.M. watching their program has to be really desperate. So they don't even try to make a whole lot of sense at that hour. They just appeal to your neediness and your credit card—both of which I just happened to have handy.

Well, you can just imagine how long I lasted with those pills. After I went through the first case of Depends, I quit cold turkey. So now I'm back to being a "talking head" once again. But who knows? I'm sure if I get depressed enough, I'll take another stab at it.[6]

Maybe I'll run five miles a day. Maybe I'll take up cycling. Maybe I'll actually take my ab roller out of its box. And if all else fails, there's always 1-800-LIPOSUX.

---

6. Or better yet, let a plastic surgeon do it.

SEVENTEEN

Dressed to Be Killed:

Fashion Torture

I HAVE WORN A LOT OF TIGHT-FITTING OUTFITS over the years that I thought made me look sophisticated, glamorous, and sexy. In retrospect, a question comes to mind. How did my internal organs survive them? Talk about being a slave to fashion—some of the get-ups I've worn were just one step removed from bondage.

Case in point: My fifties bathing suit. The insanity began as far back as when I was sixteen years old. I bought a black, strapless one-piece bathing suit, made from the latest in stretchy fabrics. How I loved that suit. Back then, we called it "stunning." But my problem was that I still had a sizable layer of baby fat around my middle, so I hated the way I looked in that stunning suit. More like stunted.

I knew I had to do something—I couldn't let the baby blubber ruin the "lines" of my new suit. So in my sixteen-year-old wisdom, I decided it would be a great idea to wear my Playtex rubber girdle under my bathing suit![1] The girdle was actually a kind of panty-girdle affair, made of rubber with a fuzzy cotton lining. Just the sort of thing everyone should be wearing in hundred-degree August heat.

The good news was that it did hold in my tummy. The bad news was that it reduced my respiration rate to that of a clinically dead person's. So there I was lying out in the broiling sun in my fifties spandex suit with a rubber girdle underneath. Words like "hot" and "sweltering" just don't do the job of describing how I felt. "Cremated" comes somewhat closer.

The unforeseen part was when I got home and tried to take the girdle off. That fuzzy cotton lining had absorbed approximately ten gallons of saltwater,[2] which

---

1. I was totally sober at the time.

2. Enough to float Shamu.

caused it to cling tighter than a sausage casing. The combination of saltwater, heat, sweat, and sand bonded it to my skin like Krazy Glue. I was literally tugging and gasping for breath for over forty-five minutes before I finally got it off. And after I did, I looked inside and found a colony of sand fleas, a couple of squid, and enough seaweed to make a bowl of miso soup.

Fashionwise, the fifties should have been called "the starch era." Our moms poured bottles of it over every piece of clothing in the house. In my opinion, my mom spent way too much alone time holed up with her starch bottle and a steam iron fired up hotter than a smelting furnace. Our slacks were starched to a point where they could stand up by themselves. Then she ironed in a crease that was so sharp, it nearly amputated your legs when you walked.

The starch thing carried over into our formal wear. One item of clothing that could by itself inflict more pain than a tonsillectomy was our prom gowns made from horsehair netting.[3] But apparently, this just wasn't uncomfortable enough for us. We had to add three to six crinolines underneath. Besides starching them, we also soaked them in a sugar and water solution and dried them over an open umbrella.

---

3. Sporting the Mr. Ed label.

The deadly tandem of the gowns and crinolines shredded our nylon stockings until our legs looked like a cat's scratching post. The gowns came with "stoles" made of matching netting, too. They stretched across the bare back, covering the shoulders. And by the end of the evening, our backs were covered with more scratches than one of Marv Albert's dates.

But we weren't through torturing ourselves. No way. May I have some more, sir? We wore a long-line Merry Widow foundation garment under the gown. These were made from the same material as a tarpaulin and were stitched with whalebone "stays" all around the sides. The cups were as hard as Formica, too. The look's effect was to push the entire bustline out there like a huge launching pad.[4] Who could breathe in one of these things? Between the lack of oxygen and abrasions inflicted on us, we could have used a general anesthetic. No wonder we drank like fishes at the proms. There was no way any human being could withstand this kind of torture sober.

The starch theme was also carried out in our hairstyles. We sprayed on the really heavy lacquer that eventually took a bigger bite out of the ozone layer than Tyson took out of Holyfield. Talk about your massive

---

4. Houston, we've got cleavage.

hair. We always looked as though we were wearing football helmets. The giant beehive coif was one of the most popular styles back then. In order to maintain their top-heavy shape, we sprayed them so thoroughly, there was no chance that even one hair could fly out of place. You could stand out on a runway in the direct line of the exhaust from a 747 jetliner and your hair wouldn't move an iota.

Next came the weirdo fashions of the sixties. I like to think of it as the "spit 'n' wipe era," because everything "hot"-looking was made from vinyl. All the trendy clothes in every decade were called "hot." Literally. The fabrics back then, like vinyl, had no breathability whatsoever. Wearing one of these outfits was like being in a blast furnace.

I remember one such outfit from the sixties that really got my mojo working. Whatever that means. It consisted of black vinyl knee-high boots and a matching vinyl dress. We called the look "mod." We mod gals were totally into the Twiggy thing. She was one of the hottest models in the sixties. Her lips weighed more than she did. Enough said. It wasn't hard for us to get down to her size, because once we were encased head to toe in our vinyl outfits, they acted as portable saunas. We could sweat off ten pounds each time we did the "frug."

On the positive side, our drycleaning bills were

nonexistent. The only maintenance a vinyl ensemble required was spit and a tissue. And for really stubborn spots, a rag and bottle of 409 worked wonders.

The seventies can be summed up in one word—polyester. It was made into Nehru jackets, bell-bottoms, and peasant blouses. The material was so durable it never wore out. You could sleep for a year in a polyester outfit, and it never wrinkled. And, of course, it was bulletproof. One of the most popular items of women's clothing, the one-piece jumpsuit, was introduced on the hit TV series *The Avengers.* All the women went crazy over jumpsuits because they looked so sleek and sexy on Emma Peel.[5]

The nineties should be labeled "the jiggle era," as demonstrated by the hit TV series *Baywatch.* Everything had to be big-big-big, overblown, and jiggly. Men were totally mesmerized by Pamela Anderson Lee's giganto silicone breasts that jiggled, her huge jiggly silicone *Baywatch* pontoon lips, and her big pouffy hair. The only thing that didn't jiggle on Pam was her buns of steel, prominently displayed flanking her thong.

The hottest thing on the nineties fashion scene was separates dressing. This translated into multiple torture. A typical singles bar outfit was a bustier and a spandex

---

5. Steed looked pretty cute in hers, too.

miniskirt worn over a thong and garter belt. Add the five-inch stiletto "screw me" shoes and a waist–cinching belt and you were stylin'. My God, it was as though our bodies had been wired together. It's a wonder we didn't sit there screaming all night. Even trying to take a few steps in an outfit like this was excruciating. Our insides are still killing us, despite the fact that we wore these outfits back in 1990.

It really steams me that guys never went through the same kind of discomfort women did just to look fashionable. The worst thing they ever had to endure was some chafing from a pair of jockey briefs that had shrunk in the dryer. They never knew what it was to primp or preen or wear outrageously uncomfortable outfits just to look sexy. They never had the pleasure of choking in a girdle or having an underwire bra crush their chests.[6] The only comparable thing they ever did was stuff a sock in their pants.

Thank God the millennium is bringing us back to our senses. After twisting, compressing, and torturing our bodies for four decades, we're finally saying, "We've had it!" Forget the Lycra, the cinch belts, the vinyl, and the leather. Our main quest is comfort for our middle-aged bodies. Good-bye, Victoria's Secret, hello L. L. Bean! I, for

---

6. David Bowie was the exception.

one, have vowed that I'll never again wear jeans so tight that they keep me constipated for three days or a bra that shoves my breasts up until they block my vision.

From now on, my boobs will be pointing south . . . toward Venezuela. And no more tight belts. Pants and skirts with elasticized waists for me, baby. This and a nice baggy sweater from the Gap and I'm in heaven. And positively no more thongs. Never again will I spend my waking hours fishing that strap out of my tushie. From now on, I'm wearing those comfortable old-fashioned nylon underpants in a size big enough to accommodate four people.[7]

Hopefully by fifty, we'll finally get over ourselves. I don't care how fat I look anymore. Thank God almighty, I'm comfortable at last. They can say I'm a broad with a future behind her. That's okay—I can take it. At least now I'm able to laugh without the help of Percodan. And if I did have implants, I'd follow Pam Anderson Lee's lead and have them removed for the sake of staying alive.[8] The final liberation is when you purchase your ticket out of Hooterville.

7. Or Ted Kennedy.

8. One million men killed themselves upon hearing Pam's announcement.

EIGHTEEN

Female Hang-ups:
Fright of Flight

OU WOULD THINK THAT AFTER YEARS OF DOING IT, most women would get over their fear of flying. The statistics have been telling us for decades that it's the safest way to travel. So why are we still afraid? Especially after the age of fifty, when most of us routinely get in the car with legally blind husbands. It doesn't make sense. Men are lucky. They don't seem to have the same fears as women. They just sit back, relax, and are sawing logs long before takeoff. On the other hand, we gals never relax. We sit there dreaming up all sorts of scary doomsday scenarios. I guess it's a girl thing. No matter how many times we board that plane, we still feel we've got better odds in an Ed McMahon sweepstakes.

I admit, I've got a real thing about flying. And it's not just limited to the safety factor. I have problems with the flight attendants, the other passengers, the first class versus coach policy, the airline food, and the delays. As an author, I travel extensively promoting my books. But I still get massive butterflies in my stomach every single time—and that's before I've even left the terminal. And by the way, who thought up that word "terminal"? It creeps me out.

Each time I board my flight, I *know* this is the one doomed to crash. Everything that happens, I interpret as a bad omen—starting with the fact that they've already lost my carry-on luggage. Prior to the flight, I compulsively check out the color weather maps in *USA Today*. I want to see if we will be heading into any F5 tornadoes over Kansas that could hurl Helen Hunt's jeep or a few renegade cows into our flight path.

I also get nervous when the captain gets on the P.A. system and introduces himself and the crew. It should have a calming effect on me, but instead I'm on guard, waiting to hear him say something like "This is your captain, Fat Chance, and my copilot today is Bob Posthumous." By now I'm a wreck. I've already started to obsess about the return flight; that's the one in which my number will be up.

Also, don't put me next to the emergency exit. The crew are obligated to read to you confusing instructions about "your responsibility" if you sit in that row. Give me a break. In my panicked state, I could never figure out how to open that door. Who do they think I am anyway—MacGyver?

As soon as we taxi down the runway, I'm white-knuckling it. And it never fails. For some reason, we always end up getting stuck out there for hours. Then the first thing they do is follow the sadistic FAA guide-lines and shut off the air conditioning. Now we're stuck in a closed tin box whose temperature is approaching that of the surface of the sun.

And while we're sitting there in suspense for hours, none of the flight crew makes any kind of announce-ment about what's going on. Then the captain finally gets on the horn and says, "It's nothing—just a small leak in the hydraulics. As soon as we get our mechanic here, it will be fixed in a jiffy." What they don't tell you is that the mechanic has to be flown in from Japan. Let me tell you something. There's no such thing as a "small" problem with a hydraulic system. It's like saying

you had a "small" problem with your health—like a
major artery exploding.

So we sit on the runway, sweltering and dying of
thirst for two and a half hours. The crew won't let you
get out of your seat to use the bathroom and they don't
tell you anything.[1] It's worse torture than an EST seminar. Then in the third hour, the captain announces that
the "small" problem has been fixed and we're "next in
line" to take off.[2] So why don't I feel any better?
Because I imagine that the hydraulics were hastily fixed
with duct tape and caulking compound, that's why. I
am not assured. Somebody explain this to me. Show me
a safety video. At my age, I need a visual aid.

No matter how calm and clear the skies are when
you depart, expect to hit turbulence halfway through
the movie. At the first bump, I've got my little window
shade up in a flash, blinding the other passengers. But I
don't care. I need to check out the huge black thun-
derclouds looming ahead so I can really start freaking
out. That's when the captain announces in his controlled but strained voice, "Fasten your seat belts—we're
in a for a bit of a chop." Geez Louise. I hate it when he
says that. "Bit of a chop" translated means the hell with

---

1. If you know too much, they'll have to kill you.

2. Approximately 107 planes ahead of you.

the seat belt. The first thing you'll need to securely fasten is your Depend. And while you're at it, polygrip your dentures down, too.

My stomach immediately settles in my mouth, and I'm hanging on for dear life for the rest of the trip.[3] I look around and notice that everyone else is sleeping, chatting, or playing cards. But that doesn't make me feel any better. I tell myself to buck up. I'm a survivor. After all, I've survived war, disease, and six seasons of *Designing Women*.

Now, I check out the expressions of the flight crew, searching for telltale signs of panic on their faces. And God help me, if any one of them is out of sorts for any reason. A common cold would be translated by me to mean that all four engines are on fire and it's just a matter of time until we're bailing out on the emergency slide. I remember where, in the safety instructions from hell, it says, "Should the cabin lose pressure, the oxygen masks will drop from the ceiling. Fasten the mask securely around your mouth." No way, lady. I'm guzzling the rest of my complimentary champagne. If I'm going down, it's going to be with as much booze in me as possible.

In the unlikely event that the flight is smooth, you can bet the farm that I'll find something else to obsess

---

3. The same physiological reaction you have during a gyno exam.

about. This takes the form of scrutinizing my fellow passengers to figure out which ones are carrying concealed bombs or weapons. Each briefcase looks incredibly suspicious to me. I'm positive that at least one harbors plastic explosives. I don't trust anyone that looks even remotely like Usama Bin Laden, Saddam Hussein, or Gary Busey. This includes people with beads of perspiration on their foreheads or wearing fake-looking beards[4] or turbans with metal canisters attached.

It doesn't take much, either, for the flight attendants to get on my nerves. If they're not way too cute, they are so old they have to keep sniffing oxygen from their demonstration masks. I also hate the ones with attitude who blow you off because they're just too busy to answer your frivolous request, such as begging for a meal three hours into the flight. When you finally get served, the food is so bad, you reckon if it had been offered to the Donner party they still would have eaten each other.

Flight attendants also get totally absorbed with trying to get the beverage cart down the aisle. Invariably, they'll roll it right over your foot if you're in the aisle seat. They never say, "I'm sorry" but instead give you a safety lecture as if you were a schoolkid about how you should keep your arms and legs out of the aisle. Well,

4. Women included.

excuse me, Mrs. Nader, but maybe the fact that my seat isn't wide enough to fit Kate Moss's skinny butt into it might have something to do with it.

The really attractive flight attendants[5] always pay way more attention to my husband than to me. They gladly supply him with extra Cokes, peanuts, and Mrs. Fields cookies. And *moi*? I get a cold dinner and a cold shoulder. So I sit there getting more and more steamed at him, because he's obviously enjoying all the attention he's getting from her. She is a knockout, though—I'll give her that. But is it too much for me to expect him to sit there passively and stop acting so flattered? I guess so. After all, she's got a butt that would make Gandhi throw in the towel.

It further aggravates me that the folks in first class are having a lot more fun than we are. I want to be part of that world. All the movie stars, CEOs, and cool people are sitting in first class. I'm tired of being stuck in coach with all the mentally unstable, the terrorists, and the guy who gets drunk and uses the beverage cart as a lavatory.

Upon reaching our destination, I'm more than ready to exit the plane. I'm first to open the overhead bin—and promptly get pummeled with everybody's junk, which has been jostling around up there like clothes in a dryer.

5. Formerly known as "stewardesses," "stews," or "Hey, baby."

People pack those bins *instead* of their suitcases. You can get hit with dishes, clothes, pets, stowaways—you name it. As far as I'm concerned, the whole experience of flying amounts to one giant survival course.

The minute I get off the aircraft, I can feel my body relaxing. But not so fast—part *deux* of my "dodging death" ordeal is about to begin when I step into a New York taxicab. The driver is not only wearing a turban but is visibly agitated and armed. Fuggedaboudit.

NINETEEN

Common Compulsions:

I'm Cleaning As Fast As I Can

BELIEVE IT OR NOT, one of the wildest fantasies common to all women has nothing to do with sex. You heard me right. It's a fantasy about having a sparkling clean house with everything in its place. A home that never gets dirty or messed up. By now you're

thinking, this fantasy would more accurately be identified as a psychotic episode. Whatever. But the reality is
that no matter how neat and clean you can possibly
make your house, it'll get messed up faster than the
speed of light when your husband and kids get home.
It's been that way since women were cleaning their
caves. But we persevere. Like Don Quixote, we're
obsessed with attaining that impossible dream even
though it always ends up a nightmare.

I wasn't always a "neat freak." Quite the contrary. I
was a total slob all the way through high school and college. Oscar Madison had nothing on me. My bedroom
was such a disaster that my mother would close my door
for weeks at a time, afraid she'd go berserk after just one
look. Thank God she chose a sensible course of inac-
tion—otherwise she'd have become hopelessly addicted
to Valium by the time I went to college.

Once a month we'd have a big showdown and my
mom would order me to clean up my room or be
grounded. I know she didn't enjoy having to punish me,
but she didn't have any other choice. If we'd had more
money, she would have called in a professional.[1]

Unfortunately, things didn't change when I went
off to college. I was still a slob. When I'd return to my

---

1. An exorcist.

room after class, I would frequently find subtle notes left on my bed by my dorm-mates that said things like *"Clean up this mess or die, bitch."*

Picky, picky, picky.

IT WAS ONLY AFTER I GOT MARRIED that I developed my obsessive-compulsive side. I guess it's a hormone thing that gives women such a powerful urge to disinfect and deodorize everything in their paths.[2] It's a primal force, stronger than the urge to procreate. How many times have we awakened in the middle of the night and gotten up to clean out our closets? How many times to have sex? I rest my case.

My family would know when I got into serious cleaning "heat" when I appeared at the breakfast table wearing rubber gloves, carrying a huge bottle of Clorox, and sporting a grout brush behind each ear. Watch out! That grout brush was always the tipoff that I had entered my "maniac mode." I was cleaning at a molecular level now. In my frenzied state, I was even capable of removing all visible stains from the Colosseum.

First stop: The fridge. When your kids are home, the refrigerator becomes a repository for all substances that are animal, vegetable, or mineral. This means you might

---

2. Including husbands and kids and in-laws.

find anything from pet hamsters to pet rocks in there. Even weirder, my boys used to keep little bags of fertilizer and chemicals from their chemistry lab on the refrigerator shelves. And if I tried to clean them out of there, they'd retaliate by leaving a homemade bomb in my cleaning bucket.

No matter how hard I tried to keep the refrigerator neatly organized, the kids could always find a secret place to put the leftovers they intended to eat tomorrow. I'd find Styrofoam containers from restaurants that the kids had left there in 1980. I would come across petrified sandwiches, apple juice fermented to 300 proof, and veggies that had such severe freezer burn, they needed skin grafts. But the worst was the six-month-old fruit that was overgrown with colonies of mold and mildew so huge, they'd capture and ingest small animals.

So, I usually tackle the job of cleaning my refrigerator with an acetylene torch and a protective body suit like the one Dustin Hoffman wore in *Outbreak*. The fumes from rotting food can get pretty strong. Also, I have no idea what kind of airborne germs are being cultured in those leftovers. It's anybody's guess what mutated life forms are lurking in there. And what if they're breeding? One day, I expect to open the door and have a creature like the *Alien* pop out at me.

Second stop: The laundry room. I am truly a self-proclaimed expert on this subject. Martha Stewart, hang up your fabric sheets.[3] I have appointed myself the official "laundry queen" because I wash clothes every single day. I can't stand to see anything sitting in my dirty-clothes hamper for more than twenty-four hours. Yeah, I know I need therapy. But so do half the women in this country who are just like me. I admit it. I get a really perverse pleasure from scrubbing out collar stains with a toothbrush, presoaking loads, and separating work clothes from delicate fabrics.

One thing I have learned from experience is, never let your husband anywhere near the laundry room. No matter how incapacitated you may be, drag yourself to that washing machine and force yourself to put in a load. Believe me, you're going to feel a lot sicker if your husband gets there first. Guys don't have a clue as to the nature of cleanliness. If left alone, they'll only wash the dirty part of the sock. And that's only after turning them inside out for a second wearing, too.

Remember, they are *guys.* We're dealing with the shallow end of the gene pool here. This, plus the fact that most of them are born color-blind. So they unwittingly mix the dark and light clothes together and then

---

3. Also, those capri pants you wore to the White House state dinner.

proceed to wash them all in *hot* water. Du-uh-uh. You can always tell the bachelors. Everything they wear is the same shade of gray. And fabric type? Forget it. A man will wash your best silk nightgown in a load along with his car towels. And just before he adds two cups of Clorox to the load with your best black crêpe-de-chine blouse, he'll use it to wipe off his lawnmower first.

I must boast that when I put a pair of socks in the dryer, they always emerge as a pair. Impressive, huh? What's my secret? It's my little obsessive-compulsive zippered net laundry bag, which keeps socks mated for life. At my age, you get your thrills where you can. And don't let your husband get within a hundred feet of the dryer. Men only dry everything at one temperature—scorching. No matter what size the clothes are when he puts them in there, they all come out a size 2. Men also have no idea, basically, about the kinds of things that should go into a dryer. They'll try to tumble-dry anything from shoes with cleats to sporting equipment. Call them uninformed. Call them idiots. But call a repairman first.

Third stop: The closets. One of women's most rewarding chores is to clean and straighten their closets. Could this be directly related to our compulsive shopping? You bet. Over the years, we've acquired more outfits than Barbie. We have fat clothes, skinny clothes, and in-between clothes. We own hundreds of items of clothing that beg to be grouped in color-coordinated order. This is such a girl thing. Only women understand the difference between beige, off-white, and eggshell.

Ditto for shoes. Yes, we absolutely have to have the same style in a dozen different colors. It's a comfort thing, like food. We also never throw anything out, because— you got it—you never know when it's going to come back into style. We have clothes in our closets that have been around since the first episode of *I Love Lucy.*

Fourth stop: The bathroom. The job of scrubbing a bathroom is about as welcome as a yeast infection. But our biggest enemy is not bacteria, mold, or those pesky silverfish bugs. It's the men in our homes who can't comprehend how to rinse five days of beard shavings and other guy gunk out of the sink. Not to mention their hairballs in the shower drain, which could trap small rodents. And for the life of them, guys of any age have still not learned how to aim straight. They always miss the toilet bowl and leave nasty dribble stains all around the bottom of the fixture. What do we have to do, paint a bull's eye in there?

Also, in order to prevent the triggering of their gag reflex, many women have to enter their bathrooms wearing gas masks to protect themselves from the time-released burritos their husbands had the night before.

Honestly, we should be awarded the Medal of Honor for being gassed in the line of duty.

The bathroom brings out, pardon my pun, the anal-retentiveness in the best of us. This is especially true when I'm away from home and have to use a public restroom. For example, I always tear off the top sheet of toilet paper on the roll. There's no way I'm going to let a sheet that's been handled by a stranger make contact with my tushie. Especially when I check out the punk rocker gal standing ahead of me in line with her spiky hair, ripped fishnet stockings, and pierced nostril. I certainly don't want any toilet paper that has made contact with *her* hands. God only knows where they've been. Men are always amazed about the length of time it takes women to go to the ladies' room. They think we must be gossiping in there. Not true. They have no idea how hard it is to use a bathroom without touching anything.

Last stop: The floors. Ah, yes! The welcome look of newly made vacuum tracks in carpet pile. The piney smell of Mr. Clean on the scrubbed tile. The slippery finish of a freshly waxed floor. Ooooow—the pain of a broken back. Somebody help me. I've fallen and I can't get up. But that's okay. I don't mind lying here for a few hours on my sparkling clean floor. I could even eat off it.

And while I'm down here, I'll try to devise clever ways to keep my house safe from my kids and husband.

Should I install gates in all the doorways? Cover all the furniture in plastic? Hire a cleaning Nazi? Then I realize there's just no way I can keep my house clean for more than five minutes at a time. What a depressing thought. It makes me want to just lie here and sniff a few aerosol cans.

TWENTY

Buying Bulk:
Trendy Gyms

I T'S OFFICIAL. The entire country has become fitness-crazed. Oh, great. Just what we need. Another area for obsessive-compulsive behavior to cripple our lives even more. Nowadays, the fitness thing isn't just limited to young people. There are eighty-year-olds out there running marathons. If I even *think* about trying to run a twenty-six-mile marathon, I start to hyperventilate. Right now, I don't have the kind of stamina it takes to watch one on TV. But I know I've got to get into some kind of exercise routine. I've got buns of mayonnaise, not steel. And with all the emphasis on cardiovascular fitness, I don't even want to guess what kind of condition my heart is in. I just heard the shocking news that Elton John got a pacemaker.[1] Who's next?

I have no excuse for sitting around growing mushier by the day. My neighborhood has a bunch of trendy gyms popping up faster than teenage zits. They're all in heated competition with each other, too. Each one tries to come up with a newer, hotter, more results-oriented kind of exercise program than the others'. So I decided to sample each program before committing to one gym. But it's a lot of pressure. Those lean and hungry sales muscle-heads stalk you from every corner. These bulked-up pinhead guys can be very intimidating with their fire and brimstone lectures about the necessity for a lifetime commitment. Cut me some slack. I only want to join a gym—not get married. I was totally unenlightened about the vast variety of exercise programs out there. When somebody told me about Pilates, I thought he was referring to a Greek statesman. And when I heard about spinning, I pictured myself strapped to a wheel, wearing nothing but a Dramamine patch. Naked I could handle. But the patch, forget it. I'm

---

1. Even more shocking than the news that he's $200 million in debt.

already maxed out on Nicoderm. Kick boxing? Doesn't that give you bad bruises on your shins? Nothing sounded enticing to me. What do you want from a middle-aged woman whose principal exercise is a rigorous session of tooth flossing?

Kick boxing: This is one of the hottest and most rapidly growing sports in America. Different gyms offer variations with different names, like the exceedingly popular Tae-Bo, created by Billy Blanks. The man is so hot right now he needs Premarin. You can't turn on the TV without seeing his infomercial or walk down an aisle in Costco without falling over a stack of his tapes. Banzai. His cardio-kick-boxing regimen combines a lot of upper-body boxing-type movements with karate-type kicks. The people taking his classes pant and sweat more intensely than the audience for a Showtime adult feature.

I tried the class and felt the only result I got was, basically, dislocating both hip joints and slipping a dozen disks. Rather than spend most of my life in frustration, not to mention traction, I tried a knockoff class called boxing aerobics. It's similar to kick boxing, except your legs don't end up in separate zip codes.[2] The instructor was a knockoff of Billy Blanks, too. His

---

2. Like on a date.

name is Joseph and he has one of the most incredible physiques I've ever seen. Like a marine drill sergeant's. He's a beautiful, hunky black guy with bulging biceps, a teeny-tiny waist, and calf muscles the size of full-grown Holsteins. Beef on the hoof, baby.

I find it really funny that our totally hip instructor teaches a class of white-bread suburban housewives like me. And we're all getting indoctrinated into the hard-core gangsta rap music he plays during classes. This is not your pussy, bubble-gum rap, either. We're talking bona fide boyz-in-the-hood stuff, booming out at two thousand decibels over the gym's monster speakers. So here we are, a bunch of women with bodies like the Pillsbury Dough Boy's, punching, prancing, and jumping rope to jive lyrics like "Kill Dat Mutha' Cop" repeated over and over again for the better part of an hour.

But I must say, we all really get into it. As Joseph calls out the moves, we sweat, groove, and really get down with it. Picture a harem of fifty women close to exhaustion who obey every command he gives like a bunch of eager puppies. I know most of our husbands would like to know why we'd never follow orders like that from them. But it's a no-brainer. When they get to be 180 pounds of trim, taut, glistening muscle, we'll consider it.

We're being transformed, little by little, into cool sisters with hot bodies. I may not ever get that good at cardio-boxing, but I'm becoming one hell of a rapper. I go home and say things to my husband like "Hi, bro. What the dealio? I been at the gym gettin' down wif my peeps. Keepin' it real in the feel." By the way, the man is close to slitting his throat. One day I expect that all the women in my class are going to get so hip that our hair will Jheri-Kurl right there on the spot.

Spinning: This exercise is truly a shock to the system. It must have been thought up by the same guy who designed the electric chair. Spinning is an intensive workout that will jump-start your metabolism faster than a Sears Die Hard battery. Performed on a stationary bicycle, this is one tour de force that would make even Lance Armstrong toss his biker shorts into the ring. The class is divided into several timed intervals in which you pedal at various speeds and resistance. By the end of twenty minutes you're wringing wet. You can actually lose up to three pounds per class. A word of caution: Many women get so skinny by the end of the week, they can slip right through their spokes and never be seen again.

Power step: This is not just your ordinary garden-variety kind of step-aerobics class. Power step pushes you to the limits of cardio conditioning—and then some. The devotees just can't get enough. Many of them pile up the platforms under their steps so high, they suffer nosebleeds up there. And you don't just step up and down. No way. That's for wusses. The idea is to leap and spring up and down during each step, as if you've got mattress coils attached to the bottom of your shoes.[3] At this level of intensity, your butt is dragging down around your ankles. This is when the instructor yells, "Let's see some energy!" Mercy. So you hop a little higher and hope you don't fall off your step. Twenty stories is a long way down.

High-impact aerobics: This was the regimen I liked the best. God only knows why. I guess I was beaten senseless by all those boxing classes before I got to this one. The gym I chose offered classes in high-impact at either 7 A.M. or 6 P.M. Thanks a lot for the accommodation, guys. Sucko time slots. I hate getting up that early. One day when I did, I realized halfway through class that I was wearing two different colored socks and my sports bra was inside out. It wasn't my fault. Who can function at 7 A.M.? Who can even see at 7 A.M? I live in fear of the day when I take off my sweatshirt and find I have forgotten to put on my bra. That's why I'm

---

3. Or walk like Richard Simmons.

taking the 6 P.M. class. I'll do the best I can, even though the only activity I'm interested in at that time slot is going to bed.

High-impact means that both feet leave the floor at the same time. In other words, you're jumping around like a maniac for an hour. You need to have not only a strong constitution but also a strong bladder. The constant pounding and jarring can cause unwelcome accidents. One good thing is that unlike in boxing aerobics, the routines aren't potentially dangerous. About the only injury you might sustain is spraining your Kegel muscles. That and the likelihood of your flabby butt bruising the backs of your thighs when you jog in place. Aerobic exercise suits me because the routines are never boring like the treadmill or stair steppers. I have a thing about machines, anyway. I don't want to be hooked up to any of them—alive or dead.

Power pumping: This is basically a nonaerobic workout in which you lift a series of weights to tone and define muscles. In other words, it's for those who enjoy posing in front of a full-length mirror, covered with extra-virgin olive oil. If you like that steroid-enhanced look, this is the class for you. You can actually firm up in a few short months by using lighter weights and doing lots of repetitions—called "reps" in the biz. The object is to look "ripped." In my present condition, the only thing ripped about me is my gym shorts.

In this class you also learn a whole new "body lingo." By the time you're through, you'll be able to flex and identify every muscle listed in *Gray's Anatomy.* You'll work on your abs, glutes, pecs, and delts. The idea is to do a lot of reps to achieve a sleek but well-defined look. Not a "six-pack" look, as they call it. Don't be tempted to try any shortcuts to build up bulk faster. Using heavy weights won't make you look more pumped. They will, however, make you look as though you should pee standing up.

When you really get into working out, you'll need to make all the dietary changes that accompany this lifestyle. Fitness freaks are into protein shakes called "smoothies." They're made with ingredients like fruit, protein powder, tofu, and sorbet. Delicious. They go down a hell of a lot easier than Rocky's six raw eggs, I can tell you that. Also, fitness freaks don't do lunch. They do Power Bars. These things are chock full of every vitamin, mineral, and amino acid in the Solar System. They're also chock full of calories—five thousand of them. So forget the side of fries.

Another thing the body builder freakazoids are heavily into, besides full-length mirrors and Wesson Oil, is "supplements." This word can mean just about anything, too. Loosely translated, the word means "resembling Lou Ferrigno." But the one all the guys are taking is called creatine. It is supposed to build up muscle mass quickly. When their head and neck are the same width, they've reached their goal. I've got news for you. It works. There are a lot of guys in the gym who are just a brain cell away from linoleum.

TWENTY-ONE

Entertainment Costs:

Party Now, Pay Later

THE THREE BIGGEST EXPENSES in an adult male's life are purchasing a home, buying a car, and paying college tuition. Women, on the other hand, can spend the combined amount of all three for one of life's most profound events—throwing a party. You got it. Livin' *la vida loca*. And as sure as the sun rises and women have PMS, there's always an occasion to throw a party. And the female philosophy is that each party should be bigger, better, and more expensive than the one before. To do it right, expect to go into debt—like the national debt. It's not just a simple case of keeping up with the Joneses. It's more like keeping up with the Rockefellers.

The way I see it, there are four occasions when women feel it's absolutely mandatory to throw an out-and-out bash. One is a wedding shower, two is the wedding, three is when someone turns forty, and the fourth—well, technically it's a category—is every birthday their kids have. Nowadays, women put more commitment and hard work into throwing their kids' birthday parties than they put into their marriages.

It wasn't always this way. When I was a kid, my birthday parties were slim pickins. My mom would invite about ten kids for a party out in the backyard, where she'd serve Kool-Aid and cake. The entire budget for our amusements ran less than a dollar. We used burlap bags for one-legged races, old clothesline to jump rope, and tin cans to bake mud pies. The dollar went for a "pin the tail on the donkey" game. In the words of Peggy Lee, "Is that all there is?" Yessiree, Bob Cratchit. It was an event right out of the pages of Dickens.

Nowadays, the lengths we go to for our kids' birthday parties are a study in extravagance. Moms regularly host "theme parties" for the kiddies and spare no expense in fulfilling their own fantasy du jour. For these celebrations really aren't given for the kids; their main function is to impress the *adult* guests. Among the most popular themes is the Cirque du Soleil backyard extravaganza with a total production budget rivaling that of *Titanic*.

Naturally, a woman isn't capable of planning and executing one of these epics without professional assistance. So she hires a party planner at $250 an hour to make sure it's a topnotch production. The result is an event that surpasses the show under a Barnum and Bailey big top. The hostess hires roving clowns, jugglers, and guys on stilts. Then there's the de rigueur artist with a full palette of greasepaint to make up all the kiddies' faces.[1] Not to mention the magicians pulling invoices out of hats and strolling troubadours working for SAG scale. The driveway is filled with catering trucks from the most "in" place available. They proudly sport their cutesy names and advertising slogans on the sides of their vans . . . LAMBIE-PIE CATERING—WE FLEECE YOU BLIND.

But the craziest thing of all is that this epic festival is being staged for a bunch of three-year-olds who can hardly comprehend colors, much less the entertainment arranged for them. The sum total of the appreciation they have for the event begins and ends with the chocolate ice cream. But all the mothers are on alert,

---

1. Which ends up all over the expensive linen napkins.

taking notes on how they're going to outdo this affair for their own kids' next birthday.

Another event worthy of a Cecil B. De Mille epic budget is a bridal shower. The most crucial thing about having the perfect shower is not the food, wine, or decorations. It's coming up with the world's most inane bridal shower games, which your guests are forced to play. Luckily, men are never subjected to them. It's well documented that men have an innate fear of bridal showers.

One of the traditional bridal shower games is to have the guests construct and model their own wedding gowns from *toilet paper*. Anal-retentive? You betcha. Admit it. You've been to at least a dozen showers in your lifetime where you played this stupid game. Each woman is given six rolls of toilet paper and challenged to wrap it around her body, artistically draping and folding it, to create the best-looking wedding gown she can. And you can't use pins or tape. Why? Don't ask. Do you think that people who request that you wrap yourself in toilet paper are capable of any type of rational thinking? After two hours of this senseless, frustrating activity, the hostess comes around and judges all the entries. The best gown wins a prize. The prize being . . . what else? A case of toilet paper.

Another favorite bridal shower game is to have a designated person write down bits and pieces of the bride-to-be's conversation while she's opening her gifts.

Then it's read back with deletions and additions that make it into a kind of sexually suggestive wedding-night script. All the gals blush and giggle while gulping down their mimosas and finger sandwiches. And by the fifth glass, the conversation has gotten rowdier than the dialogue in *Eyes Wide Shut*.[2]

Keeping with the shower theme, let's not forget the all important baby shower. These run a pretty close second to bridal showers in the "no-brainer" department. The number one baby shower game is called the pin game.[3] Every woman is handed a safety pin, which she must attach to her blouse. Then she is told not to say the word "baby." If she does, the person talking to her can take her pin away. At the end of the party, the woman with the most pins wins a prize. No, not another pin. Probably a breast pump.

When the mom-to-be gets around to opening her presents, there is more squealing going on than at Miss Piggy's place. And speaking of pigs, a baby shower is the perfect place to pig out. Next to the nine-months-preggers guest of honor, many of the women feel they look the thinnest they have in years.

But by far the most popular type of celebration to

---

2. The performances are equally bad.

3. More appropriately called the "pinhead" game.

emerge in the last decade is the fortieth-birthday party. This party is loads of fun for those over forty, because it's their big chance to get revenge on a younger man or woman—a golden opportunity for payback time. These parties can be really lavish affairs, too. Some are black-tie events held in hotel ballrooms. But no matter how uppity they get, they are always driven right back down into the gutter with the presentation of the raunchy novelty gifts for the birthday boy or girl. These "offerings" are of utmost importance in the ceremonial rite of passage. The guests go through a great deal of time and trouble[4] to choose just the "right" gift, i.e., one that will thoroughly humiliate, embarrass, and bring the birthday honoree to his knees—just in case he's not feeling old and worthless enough already.

THE PARTYGOERS SEARCH HIGH AND LOW[5] to find gifts that are examples of base humor, in the following categories:

Sexual Category

Day-glo condoms
Any type of battery-operated marital aid

---

4. And really sleazy neighborhoods.

5. Mostly low.

Hot love oils

G-strings for ladies, padded jockstraps for men

The classic porn video *Debbie Does Dallas*

Large tube of K-Y Jelly

Autographed copy of *The Kama Sutra*

Can of WD-40

Bottle of Viagra

Copy of bestseller *Sex After Forty* (pages are blank)

Anal-Retentive Category

Box of Depends

Fleet enema

Box of Ex-Lax

Giant-size bottle of Metamucil

Gift certificate for three colonoscopies

Old-Age Category

Complimentary angioplasty

Gift basket of Dr. Scholl's products

Set of dentures

Rupture truss for men, pessary for women

Porcelana cream for liver spots

THE WOMAN'S FORTIETH-BIRTHDAY PARTY follows the same general playbook. But the most important aspect of the woman's party is the entertainment. This arrives in the form of a male stripper, who rings the doorbell dressed as a Domino's Pizza delivery boy. And for identification, embroidered on his shirt pocket is a name like PAIR-O-DICE or ROD O'STEELE. He gets his boombox blaring and wastes no time in dropping his pants.[6] The guy is one gorgeous side of beef but admittedly no rocket scientist. In fact, he needs to get naked to count to twenty-one. But who cares? He's a hunka' hunka' burnin' love, baybee.

Soon, he's baring all, leaving just his tantalizing "jock sock" on. At this point, the gals are hooting, hollering, and stuffing dollar bills into his coffer. By the end of the evening, they're really getting up close and personal, trying to see what else is in there besides their life savings. Most women haven't seen anything that big since Mark Wahlberg's last scene in *Boogie Nights.*

After the female party animals crack open their sixth bottle of champagne, just about anybody would look good to them. There ought to be a warning label on the bottle, to the effect that after a few drinks, a man may appear better-looking than he actually is. (Which is probably good news to the husbands.) Party on, gals.

---

6. Velcro tear-aways.

TWENTY-TWO

Yardstick of Aging:

The Crow's Foot

WHAT DO YOU THINK is the number one concern of all women in America? Crime? Poverty? Health care? Who Clinton is currently shagging? With the possible exception of the last, none of the above. The answer is, getting older. We women are absolutely obsessed with it. Unfortunately, we live in a society that puts old age in the same general category as leprosy. I've even overheard eighteen-year-old girls complaining about frown lines, saggy butts, and crow's feet.[1]

I think the biggest culprits responsible for perpetuating this obsession with aging are the modeling agencies. They paint the faces of nine-year-olds, photograph them in seductive poses, and pay them small fortunes. These prepubescent young things are barely out of their diapers before the adults have them harnessed into sexy bustiers and skulking down the catwalks. Then at the ripe old age of twenty-five, they're washed up.

And sadly, all the women in America seem to be buying into this. It's public knowledge that these young models often turn to drugs and alcohol after their short careers are over and society throws them away in the prime of their lives. Is this the message we want sent to young women? If we've outlived our usefulness by twenty-five, what will society have in mind for us at forty? Mandatory execution?

Take that gorgeous blonde model Kim Alexis. She's probably barely forty but is already considered too old for fashion magazines or runway modeling. So what options are there for this beautiful woman? What does the moronic advertising industry allow her to do at her advanced age? Well, it's pretty bad. They have her doing

---

1. On Britney Spears.

TV commercials, singing the praises of Preparation H, Monistat, and Cortaid. With all these ailments, the poor thing must spend all her time itching, burning, and scratching.

So what's left for women older than forty? What are they allowed to speak out for? The sad truth is that the more mature personalities are reduced to doing commercials for denture and incontinence products. Gee, thanks, guys. How glamorous. We can catch the likes of perky little June Allyson pitching Depends and Florence Henderson hawking denture grip. Give me a break. Is this what we have to look forward to? Every time someone cracks a good joke we'll lose our water *and* our teeth? Spare me. I'd sooner O.D. on my prune juice.

And while we're on the subject of prune juice, it seems like the entire advertising industry is focused on the state of middle-aged colons. There must be over a hundred kinds of bran cereal on the market. Everywhere you turn, you see ads for laxatives and fiber additives. You might say we're living in a bowel-intensive society. Nowadays, many people are caught up in the fad of having a high colonic during their lunch hour.[2]

The minute we turn on TV, we're subjected to a slew of tasteless ads for hemorrhoid preparations. Have

---

2. Called a "high-nooner."

you seen the one with the young gal squirming around in her seat at a baseball game, with an agonized look on her face? You know it can only mean one thing—and it's not that her kid's team is losing the game. It's her itching and burning hemorrhoids. In my opinion, this gal looks way too young even to know what a hemorrhoid is. Also, I don't understand the logic in what she's saying. If four out of five people suffer from hemorrhoids, does that mean that one person enjoys it?

Another frequently targeted area of the older population is our reproductive organs. In our society an attitude of mourning for menopausal women because we can't have children anymore is common. Is this really a bad thing? Isn't it the normal consequence of aging? I think so. But I must be in the minority because no one else seems to accept it. We have fertility doctors working like crazy to perfect techniques that enable menopausal women to have children. Does this make sense? What woman in her right mind wants to attend her kid's elementary school graduation wearing orthopedic shoes and a hearing aid? I have enough trouble at my age just keeping my plants alive. A kid is definitely out of the question.

Am I crazy or has the whole world lost its senses? We have poured millions of our medical dollars into fertility research. Why? So the doctors can pump us full of hormones and implant us with fertilized eggs that were previously frozen? They did this to a sixty-three-year-old woman from California. Is she nuts? Why would anybody want to have a child at sixty-three years of age? For that matter, who wants to have sex at sixty-three years of age?

Another thing I don't understand is why the whole world is so interested in the flagging sex lives of fifty-year-olds. What's the big deal? It's perfectly natural for our sex drives to decrease as we get older. But for some reason, we act like it's our worst personal tragedy. Things have gotten so desperate, they've got Bob Dole pitching Viagra and talking about his sexual dysfunction on the public airwaves. Honestly, Bob, this is really more than I wanted to know about you. Anyway, I don't think Bob Dole's sexual dysfunction is our number one national problem. At his age, I think we should be more concerned about whether he's thinking about running for president again.

I guess about the only things we have to look forward to in our old age are getting geezer mail[3] and taking cruises for senior citizens. Have you ever been on one of those cruises? The average age is dead. It looks like a *Weekend at Bernie's* with all the oldies bundled in blankets and propped up in their deck chairs. You expect the staff to go around holding a mirror under

---

3. Or e-mail at www.geezer.com.

the passengers' noses to see if they're still breathing. I also don't relish the thought of playing shuffleboard with a bunch of people who have just had their hips replaced, or of dancing with an eighty-five-year-old who thinks he's the Archduke Ferdinand.[4]

Actually, the cruise lines have been getting a lot of bad press lately. They're either reporting Legionnaires' disease or poisoning all the passengers with ptomaine-laden shrimp cocktails. Not only that, but it seems like we're always reading about the ships catching fire some-place, like in the middle of the Bering Sea. I don't care how much they're touted as luxury liners, they always seem to manage to expose passengers to a life-threatening problem.

But the latest concern isn't sinking or getting sick. It's sexual harassment. Recently, a scandal broke out when it was reported that the employees of a cruise ship were indicted for sexually molesting and harassing the passengers. The truth was that during the past year, more people went down on Carnival Cruise Lines than on the *Titanic*.

SO, GIRLS, WHAT EXACTLY CAN WE DO about this aging thing? Are we doomed to sitting in front of the TV passively watching *The Price Is Right* and throwing back

---

4. Or the Queen Mum.

Ensure shooters? Not me. Okay, I accept that I'm too old to be a runway model. Nobody wants to look at an old lady strolling down the catwalk wearing her underwear outside her jeans.

And thank goodness I don't have any desire to be a mom all over again. Mother Nature is no dope. What she's perfectly prepared us to be at this age is a grandma. And believe me, it's the best of all worlds. Being a grandma means you can experience the joys of motherhood all over again without having the twenty-four-hour-a-day workload. Your new mission in life is to seek out and buy dozens of the cutest designer baby outfits ever made. We also have the time to leisurely read story after story to our grandkids and play games with them for hours on end. We can even hug them all day long, if we want.

I'm here to tell you that I, for one, give my granddaughter total unconditional love. There's *nothing* I wouldn't do for her. And I mean *nothing*. Ooops, I take it back. The minute she messes her diapers, the kid gets handed back to her parents and I'm outta there. This grandma thing is the best!

TWENTY-THREE

The NASA Syndrome:
I Need Space

I LOVE BEING MARRIED. Honest I do. My husband and I have been married for many years. We have children together. We work together. We sleep together. We eat lunch together. We take vacations together. Idyllic? Not so fast. All this togetherness is killing me! I know this sounds familiar to most women. This is why it is imperative to take at least a few "mental health" days away from our husbands and kids every year.

The thing is, most husbands don't even remotely

understand our need for space. They take it personally as a major rejection. And if we even broach the subject of having a night out with the girls, they become whiny and needy, and they all say the same thing: "Do you mean you have a better time with the girls than with me?" *Warning:* Treat this as a rhetorical question. Don't answer it under any circumstances. Take the fifth. It's really too complicated to explain, but we aren't looking for other men. We aren't exactly bored with our husbands—but we *do* have a better time with the girls.

Girls have a total blast together. What do we do that's so great? Let's start with my personal favorite, the girls' getaway. This occurs when a group of women rent a cottage at the beach for an intensive week of girl bonding.

Space, Part One: The Beach Cottage

Women consider this *the* number one most fun and therapeutic of all the getaways they can negotiate. What it amounts to is a seven-day extended slumber party for grown women. Sleep? No. Fun? Yes. This is truly the female bonding process at its most intense. It also makes our husbands crazy. They absolutely can't fathom why we would want to spend a week away from them, our homes, and the kids.[1] They want to know what the "big

---

1. Du-uh-uh.

attraction" is for us. What's so great about spending a week with a bunch of women in a small rented cottage? I'll tell you what's so great about it: *everything.* Okay, here goes. I'll list the best of the best in terms of our week-long activities:

Activity 1—grooming each other: When a group of females get together, we immediately resort to primate behavior. The focus of our day is to sit around grooming each other. This includes painting each other's toenails with wild summer shades; coloring, cutting, and styling each other's hair; and waxing each other's legs. And that's just for openers. We get silly watching each other pluck chin hairs and advising each other how to avoid bikini bumps. This is girl stuff distilled to its purest form. Like inhaling pure estrogen.

Who else are you going to talk to about such personal things? Your mother? Your kids? I don't think so. Who else but another woman your age would even begin to comprehend issues like waxing versus electrolysis or to douche or not to douche?[2] Women, by their nature, have a lot more body parts to talk about than men do. We discuss our boobs and which Victoria's Secret bras give the best cleavage.

---

2. RuPaul, perhaps.

We discuss our legs and evaluate the latest DKNY stockings for the best shades. We also update each other on the latest products in feminine hygiene. There's an awful lot to talk about, so we need at least a week.

Guys don't get it because about the only comparable thing they have to discuss is their jock itch. But we women—we're all in this together. We're not only sharing our house and clothes for the week but each other's souls too. It's like when you share your body with your child for nine months.

Activity 2—guy watching: Let's get one thing straight. All we do is *watch*—nothing more. But it sure is fun. We line up our lounge chairs on the beach and ogle the steady parade of boy-toys strutting their buff-stuff and flexing their muscles. Now I'm not going to lie. We're all hoping for some sort of catastrophic Speedo accident to occur, so we can get a peek at the goods. In the stakes of stud meat, sometimes you win, and sometimes you lose. But it's "payback time," when we gals judge guys like ground beef at the supermarket.

We employ the Olympic 1-to-10 rating system. And we don't cut anybody any slack, either. If a guy has even a hint of flab around his pecs or glutes, it's an automatic 1. And if he's hung like a Tic-Tac, he's lucky to get a .3. This is summertime show-and-tell at its best. The sandal is on the other foot, baby. These guys had better suck in their guts, tense up their biceps, and pump out those buns if they expect to get a favorable score. A woman laced with a few glasses of Chardonnay and an agenda of revenge is going to hand down more merciless judgments than those given out at Nuremberg.

Activity 3—pigging out: Each night, a different woman is in charge of providing a sumptuous gourmet dinner. Yeah, sure. Are you nuts? We're on vacation, remember? Rule 1. *The kitchen is closed.* The only time we're in the kitchen is to open another bottle of wine. It's corndogs, chips, and salsa city. Make no mistake. We're talking the *bottom* of the fast-food chain here. It's a seven-day orgy of junk food, binging on Häagen-Dazs Rocky Road out of the container, and multiple Sara Lee cheesecakes.

And speaking of multiples, the cheesecake alone is the equivalent of six orgasms a day. Trust me. We're all happy campers here, satisfied down to our painted toenails.

Activity 4—drinking: This one's hard to admit. But the truth is that we gals are really into our wine. It's strictly a BYO week, even though we haven't done this since high school. Our only exercise for the week is carrying in cases of Chablis, Chardonnay, Merlot, and champagne. The wine flows freely at a beach cottage week. And we don't bring those wussy little splits either. We buy the really big sizes. How big? Bigger than Yeltsin's liver.

Phase 1 is when we start to get sloppy and tell each other how much we love each other. Phase 2 is telling each other how much we love each other's kids. Phase 3 is reached when we are totally loaded and promise to adopt each other's kids if we should suddenly die. Right. Like that's gonna happen. On second thought, if we keep drinking like this, by the end of the week the odds it could happen are pretty good.

Activity 5—playing therapist: Part of the fun of getting sloshed is discussing things we'd never discuss with anybody else on earth. There is no topic either too intimate or too out of bounds to talk about with gal-pals. And we always tell the truth. Not like guys, who lie about everything. If our sex life stinks, we say so. Then we all take turns giving advice about how to spice it up. And after our fourth glass of wine, the advice gets so hilarious we practically wet our pants.

By the end of the evening, we are all in agreement that men are immature, irresponsible, insecure, insensitive jerks.[3] They also don't know jack about what women

---

3. Those are their good points.

really feel and think. Ragging on guys is so cathartic. We don't quit until we feel entirely cleansed.[4] Then the next day, we go out on the beach and drool over them. Okay, so no one ever accused us of being the logical sex.

Space, Part Deux: Solitary Confinement

When I was young, like Macaulay Culkin I hated being home alone. As an adult, I crave it.

And when I get that rare night to go solo, what do I do? That's an easy one. I make it a "self-maintenance" night, when I have the luxury of pampering myself without any interruptions. What sorts of things do I do? Let me speak for all of us girls:

Give ourselves a smudgeless manicure and pedicure

Tweeze our eyebrows without raising bumps the size of lima beans

Shave our legs all the way up—not just to the knee

Moisturize our hair and scalp with mayonnaise

Perform feminine hygiene–type functions

Slather raw egg white on our faces

Apply self-tanning cream without making streaks like jet contrails

Give ourselves a hot bikini wax without sustaining third-degree burns

---

4. Like from a high colonic.

Steam our pores open
Loofah, loofah, loofah the night away

AFTER I'M ALL FEMINIZED AND FEELING SILKY SMOOTH, I luxuriate between cool, clean sheets. I pop the latest chick-flick into the VCR and am able to cry my eyes out without interruption. After the sobbing, I'm completely famished. Time to raid the fridge, bringing left-over Chinese cartons back to bed. When the ants and I are thoroughly satiated, I turn my attention to the phone and make long-distance calls for hours.

By 3 A.M. there's nobody left to call, so I have a cable marathon. I love to watch the reruns of the Barbara Walters specials. I want to be famous so she can make me cry. But soon I get tired of Barbara, and that old urge begins to overtake me. No, not sex. Shopping. I automatically reach for my credit cards while flipping the remote to QVC. One thing is for sure. There is no woman in the world with enough willpower to resist those slice-'n'-dicers, vegetable peelers, or vertical chicken roasters at four in the morning. Isn't that why they call us the weaker sex?

About the Author

JAN KING IS THE NATIONAL best-selling author of the hysterical book *Hormones from Hell*. Her hilarious insights on women also appear in her books *Husbands from Hell, Hormones from Hell II, PMS Crazed, Male Bashing,* and *Why Men Are Clueless*.

Jan is also the author of a humor series about aging that includes *It's Better to Be Over the Hill Than Under It,* and she has written two self-help books.

Jan was a biology teacher in an inner-city high school before she began her writing career in the 1980s with a humor column in *Women's Image* magazine.

She has been a frequent guest on national daytime TV talk shows, including *Jenny Jones, Montel, Ricki Lake, Leeza,* and the *Today* show, where she roasted Matt Lauer on his fortieth birthday with her book *40 Deal with It*.

Jan is married to publisher Mark Chutick and is the mother of two sons.